The Arabs

The Arabs
A SHORT HISTORY

PHILIP K. HITTI

With a New Introduction
by Philip S. Khoury
Dean of Humanities and Social Science
and Professor of History
Massachusetts Institute of Technology

Gateway Editions
REGNERY PUBLISHING, INC.
WASHINGTON, D.C.

Library of Congress Cataloging-in-Publication Data
Hitti, Philip Khuri, 1886–
  The Arabs : a short history / Philip K. Hitti ; with an
 introduction by Philip Khoury.
    p. cm.
  Condensation of the author's: History of the Arabs from the
 earliest times to the present.
  Includes index.
  ISBN 0-89526-706-3 (alk. paper)
  1. Arabs—History. 2. Civilization, Arab. 3. Islamic Empire—
History. I. Hitti, Philip Khuri, 1886– History of the Arabs
from the earliest times to the present. II. Title.
DS37.7.H582 1996
909'.0974927—dc20   96-23257
                     CIP

Published in the United States by
Regnery Publishing, Inc.
An Eagle Publishing Company
422 First Street, SE, Suite 300
Washington, DC 20003

Distributed to the trade by
National Book Network
4720-A Boston Way
Lanham, MD 20706

Printed on acid-free paper.
Manufactured in the United States of America
1996 Printing

Books are available in quantity for promotional or premium use. Write to Director
of Special Sales, Regnery Publishing, Inc., 422 First Street, SE, Suite 300, Washington,
DC 20003, for information on discounts and terms or call (202) 546-5005.

Contents

Introduction

I.

When *The Arabs: A Short History* was originally published in 1943, the American public had almost no appreciation of the contributions of the Arab peoples to history and civilization. The same could be said for the public's familiarity with Muslims and Islam. If educated Americans at that time had contacts with Arabs in the United States, they would have been with Christian Arabs from geographic Syria, the preponderant group of Arabs who immigrated to America before World War II.[1] These immigrants began to arrive in the late nineteenth century. They came mainly from rural and small-town backgrounds, worked as shopowners and peddlers, and were not likely to have known a great deal about the history of their region, or at least not the high cultural traditions with which *The Arabs: A Short History* is concerned. They had belonged to the popular classes and, not surprisingly, what they

---

[1] Geographic (or Greater) Syria includes contemporary Syria, Lebanon, Jordan, Israel, and Palestine.

brought with them to America were some of their popular traditions and customs.

In American colleges and universities before World War II there were few courses devoted to the history and culture of the Arabs or to Islamic civilization. Academic interest focused on philology and linguistics, which were taught in a handful of graduate programs. The situation changed dramatically as a consequence of the war. American isolationism in the international arena ended, and quite suddenly there was demand for information and knowledge on the Near and Middle East, and especially the Arabs. There was a pressing need to produce specialists for government and higher education who were conversant with the politics, economies, cultures, and societies of that increasingly vital region. There was virtually nothing of quality in English on Arab history and civilization for the newly interested to read, apart from *The Arabs: A Short History* and the magisterial book on which it is based: *History of the Arabs*.

Neither Philip K. Hitti nor his American publisher had anticipated the timeliness of *History of the Arabs* when it was published in 1937.[2] In a few years the demand began to be felt, and not only for the long, richly detailed original version but also for an abridged version that would be accessible to beginning college students and that could also serve as a history primer for American

[2] MacMillan and Company, Ltd

policymakers and foreign service officers who had no prior knowledge of the Middle East.[3] The numerous printings and revised editions of both versions are an indication of their excellent reception over the years. Indeed, their appearance heralded the beginning of the development of the Near and Middle Eastern studies field in the United States, for which Philip K. Hitti deserves much of the credit.

Philip K. Hitti was born into a Maronite[4] family in Lebanon in 1886 and was educated at the American High School and then at the American University of Beirut (known before 1920 as the Syrian Protestant College), where he took his undergraduate degree in History in 1908. He taught there for five years before traveling to the United States and attending Columbia University, which awarded him a Ph.D. in Oriental studies in 1916. He stayed on at Columbia as a lecturer in the Department of Oriental Studies until 1920, when he returned to Beirut and his undergraduate alma mater. There, he was a professor of Oriental History until Princeton offered him a regular faculty position in 1926.

At Princeton, Hitti rose through the ranks and became a chaired professor of Semitic Literature ten years after he joined the faculty. During

---

[3] *The Arabs: A Short History* is one-third the length of *History of the Arabs* and does not include the scholarly apparatus of sources and citations in a variety of languages found in the original work.

[4] Maronites are Catholics.

Introduction

World War II he directed the Army Specialized
Training Program in Arabic and Turkish. This
served as a model for the first program in Near
Eastern studies in the United States, which he
established at Princeton immediately after the
war.[5] He was also principally responsible for
building up one of the largest Arabic manuscript
collections in the West at Princeton. By his
retirement in 1954, Hitti had already trained
many of the leaders of the next generation of
Near and Middle Eastern studies scholars for an
expanding American university system. Thus the
origins of the organized academic field of Middle Eastern studies in the United States can be
traced to Hitti's career at Princeton.[6]

II.

The division of a particular region, country, or
people into distinct historical periods is a common but rarely satisfying exercise in which historians have long engaged. In *The Arabs,* Philip K.
Hitti concentrated on the first eight centuries of
Islamic history, from the seventh until the fifteenth centuries A.D. Of these, he clearly
favored the first three or four centuries when he

[5] The Princeton program adopted the term Near Eastern
rather than Middle Eastern.

[6] For a biographical sketch of Hitti's life and career, and for
a bibliography of his publications, see James Kritzeck and R.
Bayly Winder, eds., *The World of Islam* (London: MacMillan,
1959).

Introduction

felt the Arabs enjoyed their most creative period of political and cultural achievement. During this period, the main doctrines and institutions of Islam were developed and put into practice and the Arabic language unified political and cultural life across the Middle East and North Africa. Hitti adopted for these early centuries the organizing theme of the three Arab conquests: the political and military conquest by the Arabs of western Arabia of the Middle East and North Africa; the parallel religious conquest of this vast region, which became predominantly Muslim; and the linguistic conquest by the Arabic language, which also served to unify and integrate the disparate cultures and peoples inhabiting the region.

Hitti does not adopt a central organizing theme for the second period covered by his book, from the late tenth century until the end of the fifteenth century, because the political and cultural fragmentation which characterized this period did not permit it. By then, Arab–Islamic cultural capitals had proliferated; in addition to Baghdad—seat of the most powerful and far-reaching Islamic state in the first period—there were Cairo and Cordova. A distinct political division had occurred between the major religious denominations in Islam: Sunni or majoritarian Islam and Shiite or minoritarian Islam. And the cultural dominance of the Arabic language had gradually become diluted by Persian. The military success of the Crusades in the Middle East, beginning in the eleventh century, was

xi

believed to be if not a significant contributor to this fragmentation then at least a clear reflection of it. Hitti rightly asserts, however, that the Crusades meant much more to European Christians than to the Arabs and other Muslims in the Middle East, who were more concerned with the mounting challenge posed by Turkish tribes on the eastern periphery of the region.

While Hitti was unable to construct his entire historical narrative of the Arab peoples around a single organizing theme, he did adopt several sub-themes which are crucial to his story. Two deserve special mention: the first is the degree to which Arab Muslims tolerated non-Arabs and non-Muslims generally; the other concerns the evolution of the Arabic language, how it shaped and reflected the identity of the Arab peoples, and its enormous power as a cultural unifier.

Hitti points out that under Arab-Muslim rule, non-Muslims faced various forms of discrimination. Slavery existed, though conversion to Islam could result in manumission. And there were at least two kinds of slaves: chattel slaves and slaves who constituted military elites and who came to govern vast parts of the Middle East and North Africa for significant periods of time in the later Middle Ages and in early modern times. Arab Muslims were not slaves, however. At times, Christians and Jews were required to wear special dress, and in courts of law their testimony against a Muslim would not be accepted; but, because they were recognized as "people of the scripture" under Islam, they could worship freely in their own churches and temples, engage in commerce and finance, practice the professions, and accumulate wealth. In the early centuries of Islam, and in later periods as well, they were the leading traders in the Middle East. Occasionally, they also held high public office. In return for "protection," they had to pay a special tax, from which Muslims were exempt. On balance, Hitti finds that Jews fared better than Christians under Arab–Muslim rule, and that Jews under Arab–Muslim rule fared better than Jews under Christian rule in Europe during the Middle Ages.

Hitti's academic roots in the Orientalist tradition of philology are in evidence throughout *The Arabs.* He does not conceal his admiration for Arabic poetry, especially that of the court poets at Damascus and Baghdad who were known for their libidinous verse. He exalts in demonstrating how certain common English terms derived from Arabic. He is especially keen on tracing the derivation of scientific and medical terms, though he also finds other interesting examples: for instance, the origin of the term for the sport of tennis "probably" came from Tinnis, a village in Egypt which produced linen used in the making of tennis balls (page 128). More importantly, Hitti considers the evolution of Arabic from its place as the language of poetry in pre-Islamic western Arabia, to its role as the language of "revelation and religion" in the early centuries of Islam, to its importance as a medium of rigorous scientific and philosophical thought. For him, the geographic spread of Arabic concomitantly widened the notion of what it meant to be an Arab. At first, Arabic was the exclusive language of the Arab tribal conquerors who poured out of western Arabia into the more culturally sophisticated Greco–Roman and Persian belts to the North, East, and West. In a matter of a few centuries Arabic had replaced Greek, Aramaic, and Persian as the language of high culture and politics; in the process it helped to dilute the racial or ethnic associations of the language with the first Muslims. Simply put, "an Arab henceforth became one who professed Islam and spoke and wrote the Arabic tongue, regardless of his racial affiliation" (page 100).

What Hitti relishes most of all are the vast array of cultural and scientific achievements that occurred during the first eight centuries of Islam and that were transmitted largely through the medium of Arabic. He makes it abundantly clear that the political, military, religious, and linguistic conquests undertaken by the Arabs made them the inheritors of the great cultural traditions associated with Greece, Rome, and Persia, and the creators of a new civilization defined by Islam. Their inheritance enabled the Arabs, among other Muslims, to recover learning and knowledge from earlier periods of history and to make new advancements and discoveries on their own. Equally important, they were to transmit much of their accumulated learning and knowledge to Europe mainly through Muslim Spain, thereby assisting in no small measure the birth of the European Renaissance. The Middle Ages, by Hitti's lights, were the halcyon days for the Arabs, the era in which they took their place on the center stage of world history, never to do so in quite the same way again.

Hitti only has space in his *Short History* to highlight the contributions of the most important historians, philosophers, and scientists, including those who made significant contributions to medicine. He points out that many were not ethnically Arab but that their most important contributions to knowledge were rendered in the Arabic language. Ibn Sina (Avicenna), the greatest Platonist of the Middle Ages and a major contributor to medical knowledge, and al-Razi (Rhazes), the brilliant surgeon, were both of Persian origin. Ibn Rushd (Averroës), the leading Aristotelian thinker of this period and a celebrated jurist, lived in Muslim Spain, which receives disproportionate attention in *The Arabs* because so much of the learning and knowledge acquired and refined in the Muslim world was transmitted to Christian Europe via Spain. Hitti also gives North Africa its due, and singles out Ibn Khaldun, the fourteenth-century jurist and philosopher of history, whom scholars in our own times have labeled the first modern sociologist. Ibn Khaldun's systematic description and analysis of how states are formed and the forces that cause their eventual disintegration is remarkable for the way it unearths patterns that can help us to understand long-term historical change.

III.

The story of the Arabs as narrated by Hitti comes to a sudden close in the fifteenth century and is not taken up again, and then only briefly, until the advent of the twentieth century. Why does Hitti pass over the four centuries of history when the Arabs lived under Ottoman Turkish rule? He is reported to have said "there was no Arab history then,"[7] and he was correct, at least in the sense that the Arabs had long before ceded political and cultural power to the other two ethnic groups that exercised massive influence on the Middle East: first the Persians, and then the Turks. Hitti, it must be remembered, was writing at a time when history meant the study of the institutions of political power and authority and the international relations of states. During four centuries of Ottoman rule (1516–1918), the Arabs enjoyed a certain measure of local and regional influence within the Ottoman Empire, but the Turks controlled the machinery of imperial government in Istanbul and the empire's international diplomacy.

Hitti may also have had another, more personal and emotional reason for treating four centuries of Arab history as if they had never existed. He had grown up and had been formed intellectually at the turn of the twentieth century, when an increasing number of Arabs from geographic

---

[7] See Albert Hourani, "Writing the History of the Middle East," *International Journal of Middle East Studies,* 23 (1991), 133.

Syria, including Lebanon, began to express a certain disillusionment with Ottoman Turkish rule. Increased Turkish oppression in the Arabic-speaking parts of the Ottoman Empire and a series of humiliating military defeats at the hands of the European Powers encouraged some to plot against the empire in which Arabs had been living for several centuries and to reassert their own Arab political rule. These were the first stirrings of modern nationalism in the Arab world. Educated Arabs in general began to construct a variety of new political identities for themselves—Lebanese, Syrian, Palestinian, Iraqi, Arab; by so doing, some categorically rejected their present circumstances and spoke of a more distant historical and even mythical past when Arabs had established one of the greatest empires in history and made significant contributions to world civilization. This dream of the past they now glorified and contrasted to their unfavorable contemporary circumstances under Turkish rule. Hitti probably harbored such sentiments towards Turkish rule, and he may have acquired them at the American University of Beirut, a hotbed of early Arab political unrest. The fact that he was a Christian from Mount Lebanon, which already enjoyed considerable autonomy but not full independence from Ottoman rule, may have discouraged him from seeing anything good or worthy in the Turks and their governance. Because he could not recount this period with pride and glory, he chose to skip over the four-hundred-year history of the Arabs in the Ottoman Empire.

Introduction

Present-day historians would have difficulty accepting Hitti's premise. Recent scholarship indicates that Ottoman Turkish rule was not as oppressive as he and other Arab intellectuals of his generation have suggested.[8] Moreover, the Turks had developed a highly organized system of administration that extended over a vast Islamic empire, facilitated trade within its borders, and promoted a relatively stable agricultural regime based on a reasonable system of taxation which also allowed urban life to flourish, in Istanbul and in the Arab provinces. And in these provinces, a thriving Ottoman–Arab elite exercised considerable local and regional influence.

In giving short shrift to the Ottoman Empire, Hitti also neglects to do justice to the impact in the long nineteenth century of an expanding Europe on the Arabs, apart from mentioning when different Arab provinces of the empire came under European control: Algeria between 1830 and 1847; Tunisia in 1881; Egypt in 1882; Libya in 1911; and geographic Syria and Iraq at the end of World War I. The rapid spread of European political power, trade and finance, and culture into the Middle East and North Africa turned significant portions of the region into a kind of plantation for Europe, and the momentous decisions on the future of the Arabs were taken in London and Paris. The Arabs had lost even more control over their own destinies than

[8] See George Antonius, *The Arab Awakening* (London: H. Hamilton, 1938).

before, and Hitti might have done more to explain this reality.

Hitti, like other historians, has increasing difficulty maintaining a healthy distance from his subject. His last chapter all too briefly mentions the collapse of the Ottoman Empire, the rise of Arab nationalism, the establishment of direct European rule over the Arabic-speaking territories of the empire, the struggles for national independence, and the creation of new states and their entry into the United Nations after World War II. There is but slight mention of the momentous events in Palestine in 1948 and what the establishment of modern Israel has meant for the Arabs. There is no mention of the Cold War, Nasser, and the rise of radical nationalist and Islamic movements. For these and subsequent events, the student will have to turn to more recent studies, of which there are many.

In the end, Hitti's beautifully told story has limitations that no single volume can overcome. He wrote it at a particular moment in time, when the United States had discovered a need for knowledge of a people about whom they were woefully ignorant. Hitti met that need but on his own terms, preferring to emphasize the major achievements of the Arabs, most of which had occurred centuries before. He exercised the right of all historians: to define his subject as he saw fit. And, like all historians, his own personal background, life experiences, intellectual formation, and formal training contributed to that defining process.

Philip K. Hitti's natural successor in the enterprise of writing the history of the Arabs noted recently that Hitti's kind of history was, on the one hand, "the careful elucidation of what may have happened on the basis of literary works written in other ages for other purposes," and yet on the other, it "was a necessary preparation for what came later."[9] This helps to explain why *The Arabs: A Short History* continues to be a valuable primer half a century after its first appearance.

PHILIP S. KHOURY
Massachusetts Institute of Technology
JULY 1996

[9] Hourani, Albert, "Writing the History of the Middle East," p. 129. In 1991, Hourani published *A History of the Arab Peoples* (Harvard University Press) to great critical acclaim. This book has not yet been abridged.

List of Maps

Preface

Events concomitant to the last two World Wars and developments in the post-war period have forced the United States into a first-rank position among the nations of the world and thrust upon its people the necessity of dealing with and understanding other peoples. Among the least understood are the Arabic-speaking people, numbering over ninety million, occupying an unbroken stretch of land—from Morocco to Iraq —that lies athwart the great international highway connecting the three historic continents, stores some of the richest oil reservoirs in the world and bristles with national and international problems upon the solution of which universal peace might well depend.

Oil in Arab lands has in recent years loomed as an increasingly important factor in the life and economy of the people and in international affairs. About two-thirds of the world's proved oil reserves lie on Arab soil. Millions upon millions of pounds sterling and of American dollars are invested in the oil industry here.

But our concern in the region is not merely political or economic. Our cultural ties with the area have preceded by generations all such contacts. They date from the second quarter of the last century when American teachers, preachers, archeologists and social workers began to flock to the eastern borders of the Mediterranean which had cradled Judaism and Christianity and contributed immeasurably in medieval times to our scientific and literary heritage. The beginnings of the third and closely-related monotheistic religion, Islam, also lay in this Arab area. It was mainly the work of those Americans, jointly with the work of British and French educators, that served to awaken the Arab East from its slumber and set it on the road of progress and modernism. The resultant intellectual renaissance contributed to the revitalization of the entire Moslem society of which the Arab community constitutes the core.

The following pages are intended to tell briefly and simply the story of these Arabic-speaking people and of their culture. It enrolls before us one of the truly magnificent and instructive panoramas of history. The contents have been distilled from the author's larger volume entitled *History of the Arabs*, published first by Macmillan in London and New York. Originally produced by Princeton University Press, *The Arabs: A Short History* has since gone through numerous editions, here and in England, and translated into a number of European and Asiatic languages including French, Spanish, Portuguese, Dutch, Arabic, Urdu and Indonesian. It is hoped that through this pocket edition, revised and brought up to date, the book will increase its usefulness as a guide to the layman and an introduction to the student.

P.K.H.

April, 1970

The Arabs

Arabs, Moslems, and Semites

One hundred years after the death of Muhammad his followers were the masters of an empire greater than that of Rome at its zenith, an empire extending from the Bay of Biscay to the Indus and the confines of China and from the Aral Sea to the lower cataracts of the Nile. The name of the prophet-son of Arabia, joined with the name of almighty Allah, was being called five times a day from thousands of minarets scattered over southwestern Europe, northern Africa and western and central Asia. In this period of unprecedented expansion, the Moslem Arabs "assimilated to their creed, speech, and even physical type, more aliens than any stock before or since, not excepting the Hellenic, the Roman, the Anglo-Saxon or the Russian."

The Babylonians, the Assyrians, the Chaldae-

1

ans, the Aramaeans, the Phoenicians—all of whose ancestors were nurtured in the Arabian peninsula—were, but are no more. The Arabs were and remain. They stand today as they stood in the past in a strategic geographical position astride one of the greatest arteries of world trade. Since the first World War these people have become increasingly conscious of their heritage and potentialities. Until the first World War all the eastern part of the Arab area lay within the embrace of the Ottoman Empire. Now Iraq, after a period of tutelage as a British mandate, is a fully independent state, having replaced its monarchy with a republic in 1958. The capital, Baghdad, is of *Arabian Nights'* fame. Lebanon, distinguished by a Christian majority of population and Westward orientation since Phoenician days, declared itself a republic when still under the French mandatory. Its capital Beirut has grown into one of the busiest and most modern cities of the Orient. Lebanon's neighbor Syria likewise freed itself from the French tutelage and established a republican form of government, with the city of Damascus, once the glorious seat of the Umayyads, as capital. The emirate of Transjordan, sponsored by the British mandate over Palestine, has since evolved into the Hashimite Kingdom of Jordan under a descendant of the Prophet Muhammad. Ibn-Saud, the strong man of modern Arabia, carved out for himself and consolidated a large kingdom—including most of central, northwestern and northeastern Arabia—the like of which Arabia has not witnessed since the days

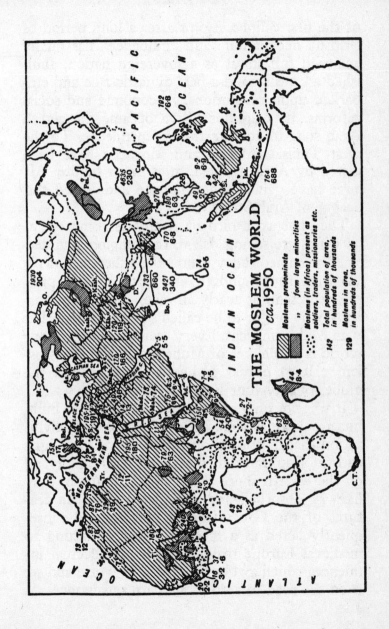

THE MOSLEM WORLD
Ca. 1950

Moslems predominate
    "   form large minorities
    "   (in Africa) present as
      soldiers, traders, missionaries etc.

142   Total population of area,
     in hundreds of thousands

120   Moslems in area,
     in hundreds of thousands

of the first caliphs. Egypt after a long period of British occupation and influence has finally achieved full status as a sovereign nation, abolished a century-and-a-half dynastic rule and embarked upon revolutionary economic and social reforms. Its neighbor Libya became the eighth Arab state to achieve full independence. To the west Tunisia, Algeria and Morocco have been stirred by Arab nationalism as never before. All three have gained independence and joined the League of Arab States.

The phoenix, a bird of Araby, is rising again. Its wings are strong. Islam, the religion founded by Muhammad today claims the adherence of no less than four hundred and fifty million people, representing nearly all races. These are Moslems, who prefer to be called by this name rather than Muhammadans. Every seventh person in our world is a follower of Muhammad, and the Moslem call to prayer is heard almost round the globe, twenty-four hours of the day.

It was not only an empire that the Arabs built, but a culture as well. Heirs of the ancient civilization that flourished on the banks of the Tigris and the Euphrates, in the valley of the Nile and on the eastern shore of the Mediterranean, they likewise absorbed and assimilated the main features of the Greco-Roman culture, and subsequently acted as a medium for transmitting to medieval Europe many of these intellectual influences which awoke the Western world and set it on the road toward its modern renaissance.

4

Arabs, Moslems, and Semites

No people in the early Middle Ages contributed to human progress so much as did the Arabs, a term which in our usage would comprise all Arabic-speaking peoples, including the Arabians, that is, the inhabitants of the Arabian peninsula. Arab scholars were studying Aristotle when Charlemagne and his lords were reportedly learning to write their names. Scientists in Cordova, with their seventeen great libraries, one alone of which included more than 400,000 volumes, enjoyed luxurious baths at a time when washing the body was considered a dangerous custom at the University of Oxford.

The story of the Arabs is of especial importance to us since at the core of it is the story of the third and latest of the world's great monotheistic religions, so closely allied to Judaism and Christianity. Historically, Islam is an offshoot of these other two, and of all faiths it comes nearest to being their kin. All three are the product of one spiritual life, the Semitic life. A faithful Moslem could with but few scruples subscribe to most of the tenets of Christian belief. The success of Arab arms waxed and waned; it was the Prophet's idea—the idea of a single God—which time and again triumphed over peoples like the Mongols and Turks, who had themselves subdued the Arabs. In 1947 a colossal Moslem state, Pakistan, with a population of some seventy millions, was born. Indonesia, with almost the same population, followed (1949). Sudan (1956), Malaysia (1963) and other states in Africa and

5

Arabia have since achieved independence. Islam has been and still is a way of life to millions of the human race.

The Arabic language today is the medium of daily expression for around one hundred million people. For several centuries it was the language of learning, culture and progressive thought throughout the civilized world. Between the ninth and twelfth centuries more works—philosophical, medical, historical, religious, astronomical and geographical—were produced through the medium of Arabic than through any other tongue. The vocabularies of European languages bear the marks of its influence. Its alphabet is, next to the Latin, the most widely used system in the world.

Of the two surviving representatives of the Semitic people, the Arabs, in a larger measure than the Jews, have preserved the characteristic physical features and mental traits of the family. Their language, though the youngest among the Semitic group from the point of view of literature, has nevertheless conserved more of the peculiarities of the mother Semitic tongue—including the inflection—than the Hebrew and its other sister languages. Islam, too, in its original form is the logical perfection of Semitic religion. In Europe and America the word "Semite" has come to have a Jewish connotation, but the "Semitic features," including the prominent nose, are not Semitic at all. They are exactly the characteristics which differentiate the Jew from the Semitic type and evidently represent an acquisi-

tion from early intermarriages between the
Hittite-Hurrians and the Hebrews.

The reasons which make the Arabian Arab,
the nomad especially, the best representative of
the Semitic family biologically, psychologically,
socially and linguistically should be sought in his
geographical isolation and in the monotonous
uniformity of desert life. Ethnic purity is a reward of a most ungrateful and isolated environment, such as central Arabia affords. The "Island
of the Arabians" furnishes an almost unique example of uninterrupted relationship between
populace and soil. If immigrations have ever
taken place into Arabia resulting in successive
waves of settlers ousting or submerging one another—as in the case of India, Greece, Italy,
England and the United States—history has left
no record of them. Nor do we know of any invader who succeeded in penetrating the sandy
barriers and establishing a permanent foothold in
this land. The people of Arabia, particularly the
Bedouins, have remained virtually the same
throughout all recorded ages. And it was in Arabia that the ancestors of the Semitic peoples—the
Babylonians, the Assyrians, the Chaldaeans, Amorites, Aramaeans, the Phoenicians, Hebrews,
Arabians and the Abyssinians—had their origin.
Here they lived at some time as one people.

If Arabia provided the original home of the
Semites, the Fertile Crescent—the region extending from the Persian Gulf to Sinai and including
Iraq, Syria, Lebanon and Palestine—was the home
of their early civilization. In the Euphrates valley

to which Semites migrated as early as the mid-fourth millennium before Christ, blossomed the early Babylonian culture, which has bequeathed to us a system of weights and measures and the sexagesimal system by which time is still measured. To North Syria went a thousand years later the Amorites, one of whose component parts were the Canaanites, called Phoenicians by the Greeks, who occupied the coast of Lebanon and became the first great colonizers and international traders. If they contributed only the alphabet, that is enough to justify including them among the greatest benefactors of humanity.

The Arabian Moslems, as a result of their phenomenal conquests, became through the Aramaeans (Syrians) heirs of these early Semites. They also inherited elements of the South Arabian culture. In Yaman the Minaeans, Sabaeans and Himyarites had founded flourishing states that endured from about 1200 B.C. to A.D. 525. The Queen of Sheba, as the name indicates, was of South Arabian origin.

The Original Arab,
the Bedouin

Although we are concerned in this book with all Arabic-speaking peoples—not only in Arabia but in many lands, including Syria, Lebanon, Palestine, Jordan, Iraq, Persia, Egypt, North Africa and medieval Sicily and Spain—it is necessary to throw the spotlight first upon the original Arab, the Bedouin.

The Bedouin is no gypsy roaming aimlessly for the sake of roaming. He represents the best adaptation of human life to desert conditions. Wherever grass grows, there he goes seeking pasture. Nomadism is as much a scientific mode of living in the Nufud as industrialism is in Detroit or Manchester. It is a reasonable and stoic adjustment to an unfriendly environment. For the surface of Arabia is almost completely desert with only a narrow strip of habitable land round the periphery. The Arabians called their habitat an island, and an island it is, surrounded by water on three sides and by sand on the fourth.

Despite its size—it is the largest peninsula in the world—its total population is estimated at only seven to eight millions. Geologists tell us that the land once formed the natural continuation of the Sahara (now separated from it by the rift of the Nile Valley and the great chasm of the Red Sea) and of the sandy belt which traverses Asia through central Persia and the Gobi Desert. It is one of the driest and hottest countries in the whole world. True, the area is sandwiched between seas on the east and west, but these bodies of water are too narrow to break the climatic continuity of the Africo-Asian rainless continental masses. The ocean on the south does bring rains, to be sure, but the monsoons (an Arabic word, incidentally) which seasonably lash the land leave very little moisture for the interior. It is easy to understand why the bracing and delightful east wind has always provided a favorite theme for Arabian poets.

The Bedouin still lives, as his forebears did, in tents of goats' or camels' hair ("houses of hair"), and grazes his sheep and goats on the same ancient pastures. Sheep-and-camel-raising, and to a lesser degree horse-breeding, hunting and raiding, are his regular occupations, and are to his mind the only occupations worthy of a man. It is his conviction that agriculture—as well as all varieties of trade and craft—are beneath his dignity. And indeed there is not much tillable land.

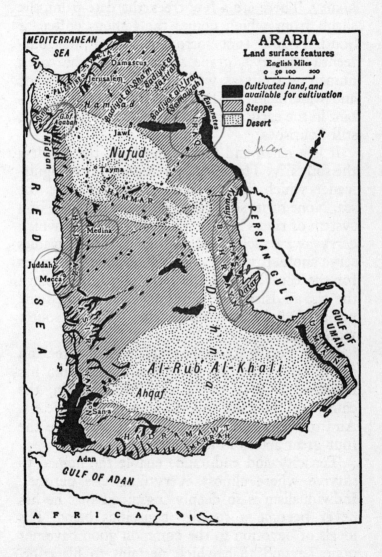

ARABIA
Land surface features
English Miles
0 50 100   300

◼ Cultivated land, and
   available for cultivation
▨ Steppe
⠿ Desert

MEDITERRANEAN
SEA

Damascus
Jerusalem

SYRIA
Badiyat al-Sha'm
Badiyat al-Jazirah
Badiyat al-'Iraq (Samawah)
Euphrates
IRAQ
PERSIAN GULF
BAHRAYN
Tuwayq
HASA
Qatar

G. of Aqaba
Midyan
Jawf
Nufud
Tayma
SHAMMAR

RED SEA

Medina

Juddah
Mecca

'ASIR

D a h n a

Al-Rub' Al-Khali

Ahqaf

Sana

HADRAMAWT
MAHRAH

Adan

GULF OF ADAN

AFRICA

'UMAN
GULF OF UMAN

Iran
N

There is little wheat. Bread, to the Arabian, is a luxury. There are a few trees, the date-palm, the shrub from which comes the famous coffee of South Arabia (not introduced until the fourteenth century), grape vines, and in the oases, numerous fruits as well as almonds, sugar cane and watermelons. The frankincense tree, important in the early commercial life of South Arabia, still flourishes.

It is a harsh and forbidding land, the air dry, the soil salty. There is not a single river of significance which flows perennially and reaches the sea. None of its streams is navigable. In place of a system of rivers it has a network of wadies which carry away such floods as occur. These wadies serve another purpose: they determine the routes for the caravans and the holy pilgrimage. Since the rise of Islam the pilgrimage has formed the principal link between Arabia and the outer world.

In the Fertile Crescent empires have come and gone, but in the barren wastes the Bedouin has remained forever the same. The Bedouin, the camel and the palm rule supreme over the desert. And together with the sand they constitute the four great actors in its drama.

Tenacity and endurance enable the nomad to survive where almost everything else perishes. Individualism is so deeply ingrained that he has never become a socially conscious being. His ideals of devotion to the common good have not gone beyond that which pertains to his tribe.

Discipline, respect for order and authority are not among his ideals.

The rudiments of Semitic religion developed in the oases, rather than in the sandy land, and centered upon stones and springs, forerunners of the Black Stone and Zamzam Well in Islam and of Bethel in the Old Testament. But religion sits very lightly in the heart of the Bedouin. In the judgment of the Koran, "the desert Arabians are most confirmed in unbelief and hypocrisy." Even in our present day they pay little more than lip homage to the Prophet.

The monotony and aridity of his desert habitat are faithfully reflected in the nomad's physical and mental make-up. He is a bundle of nerves, bones and sinews. Dates and milk are the chief items on his menu; and dates and camel flesh are his only solid foods. Fermented, the date gives him his favorite beverage. Its crushed stones furnish the cakes which are the everyday meal of his camel. To possess "the two black ones," water and dates, is the dream of every Bedouin.

His raiment is as scanty as his nourishment: a long shirt with a sash—an Arabic word—and a flowing upper garment which pictures have made familiar. The head is covered by a shawl held by a cord. Trousers are not worn and footwear is rare.

Of the animals of Arabia, two are preeminent: the camel and the horse. Without the camel the desert could not be conceived of as a habitable place. It is the nomad's nourisher, his vehicle of transportation and his medium of exchange. The dowry of the bride, the price of blood, the profit of gambling, the wealth of a sheikh—all are computed in terms of camels. It is the Bedouin's constant companion, his alter ego, his foster parent. He drinks its milk instead of water, which he spares for the cattle; he feasts on its flesh; he covers himself with its skin; he makes his tent of its hair. Its dung he uses as fuel, and its urine as a hair tonic and medicine (as shampoo it leaves on the hair an odor corresponding to perfume and on the face a layer of oil serviceable as a protection against insect bites). To him the camel is more than "the ship of the desert"; it is the special gift of Allah.

The Bedouins of our day take delight in referring to themselves as "the people of the camel." Musil, in his book on the Ruwalah Bedouins, states that there is hardly a member of that tribe who has not on some occasion drunk water from a camel's paunch. In time of emergency either an old camel is killed or a stick is thrust down its throat to make it vomit water. If the camel has been watered within a day or two, the liquid is tolerably drinkable.

As Arabia is the chief camel-breeding center of the world, the camel industry is one of its great sources of income. The part which the camel has played in the economy of Arabian life is indicated by the fact that the Arabic language is said to include about a thousand names for the camel in its numerous varieties, breeds, conditions and stages of growth, a number rivaled only by the number of synonyms used for the sword.

The horse, on the contrary, is an animal of luxury whose feeding and care constitute a problem to the man of the desert. Its possession is a presumption of wealth. Renowned as the Arabian horse has become in Moslem literature, it was nevertheless a late importation into ancient Arabia. But once there, before the beginning of our era, it had a perfect opportunity to keep its blood pure and free from admixture. Celebrated for its physical beauty, endurance, intelligence and almost touching devotion to its master, the Arabian thoroughbred is the origin from which all Western ideas about the good breeding of horseflesh have been derived. In the eighth century the Arabs introduced it into Europe through Spain, where it left permanent traces in its Barbary and Andalusian descendants. During the Crusades the English animal received fresh strains of blood from the Arabian horse.

The horse's chief value to an Arabian lies in providing the speed necessary for the success of Bedouin raids. It is also used for sports: in tournament, coursing and hunting. In an Arab camp today if there is a shortage of water the children may cry for a drink, but the master, unmoved, would pour the last drop into a pail to set before the horse.

The raid or *ghazw* (corrupted into "razzia"), otherwise considered a form of brigandage, is raised by the economic and social conditions of desert life to the rank of a national institution. It lies at the base of the economic structure of Bedouin pastoral society. In desert land, where the fighting mood is a chronic mental condition, raiding is one of the few manly occupations. Christian tribes, too, practiced it. An early poet gave expression to the guiding principle of such life in two verses: "Our business is to make raids on the enemy, on our neighbor and on our own brother, in case we find none to raid but a brother!"

According to the rules of the game—and *ghazw* is a sort of national sport—no blood should be shed except in cases of extreme necessity. *Ghazw* does help to a certain extent to keep down the number of mouths to feed, though it does not actually increase the sum total of available supplies. A weaker tribe or a sedentary settlement on the borderland may buy protection by paying tribute to the stronger tribe.

The principle of hospitality, however, mitigates in some measure the evils of *ghazw*. However dreadful he may be as an enemy, the Bedouin is also loyal and generous within his laws of friendship. Pre-Islamic poets, the journalists of their day, never tired of singing the praises of hospitality which, with fortitude and manliness, is considered one of the supreme virtues of the nation. The keen competition for water and pasturage, on which the chief causes of conflict center, splits the desert populace into warring tribes; but realization of helplessness in the face of a stubborn and malignant nature develops a feeling for the necessity of one sacred duty: that of

16

hospitality. To refuse a guest such a courtesy in a land where there are no inns or hotels, or to harm him after accepting him as a guest, is an offense not only against the established mores and honor, but against God Himself, the real protector.

The clan organization is the basis of Bedouin society. Every tent represents a family; members of one encampment constitute a clan. A number of kindred clans grouped together make a tribe. All members of the same clan consider each other as of one blood, submit to the authority of but one chief—the senior member of the clan—and use one battle-cry. Blood relationship—real or fictitious (clan kinship may be acquired by sucking a few drops of a member's blood)—furnishes the cohesive element in tribal organization.

The tent and its humble household contents are individual property, but water, pasturage and tillable land are common property of the tribe.

If a member of a clan commits murder inside the clan, none will defend him. In case of escape he becomes an outlaw. If the murder is outside the clan, a vendetta is established, and any fellow clan member may have to pay for the crime with his own life.

Blood, according to the primitive law of the desert, calls for blood; no chastisement is recognized other than that of vengeance. The nearest of kin is supposed to assume primary responsibility. A blood feud may last forty years. In all those intertribal battles of pre-Islamic days, the chroniclers emphasize the blood-feud motif, though underlying economic reasons must have motivated many of the events.

No worse calamity could befall a Bedouin than the loss of his tribal affiliation, for a tribeless man is practically helpless. His status is that of an outlaw beyond the pale of protection and safety.

The spirit of the clan demands boundless and unconditional loyalty to fellow clansmen, a passionate chauvinism. His allegiance, which is the individualism of the member magnified, assumes that his tribe is a unit by itself, self-sufficient and absolute, and regards every other tribe as its legitimate victim and object of plunder and murder. Islam made full use of the tribal system for its military purposes. It divided the army into units based on tribal lines, settled the colonists in the conquered lands in tribes, and treated new converts from among the subjugated peoples as "clients" or protégés. By a "client" Arabs ordinarily mean one who seeks voluntarily to become a member of a chosen clan. The unsocial features of individualism and the clan spirit were never outgrown by the Arab character as it developed and unfolded itself after the rise of Islam, and were among the determining factors that led to the disintegration and ultimate downfall of the various Islamic states.

The clan is represented by its titular head, the sheikh. Unlike his modern namesake of Hollywood fame, the sheikh is the senior member of the tribe whose leadership asserts itself in sober counsel, in generosity and in courage. In judicial, military and other affairs of common concern the sheikh is not the absolute authority; he must consult with the tribal council composed of the heads of the component families. His tenure of office lasts during the good will of his constituency.

The Arabian in general and the Bedouin in particular is a born democrat. He meets his sheikh on an equal footing. The society in which he lives levels everything down. The Arabian until recently never used the title *malik* (king) except in referring to foreign rulers. But the Arabian is also aristocratic as well as democratic. He looks upon himself as the embodiment of the consummate pattern of creation. To him the Arabian nation is the noblest of all nations. The civilized man, from the Bedouin's·exalted point of view, is less happy and far inferior. In the purity of his blood, his eloquence and poetry, his sword and horse, and above all his noble ancestry, the Arabian takes infinite pride. He is fond of prodigious genealogies and often traces his lineage back to Adam.

The Bedouin woman, whether Islamic or pre-Islamic, enjoyed and still enjoys a measure of freedom denied to her sedentary sister. She lived in a polygamous family and under a baal system of marriage, in which the man was the master; nevertheless she was at liberty to choose a husband and leave him if ill-treated.

Ability to assimilate other cultures when the opportunity presents itself is well marked among the children of the desert. Faculties which have

remained dormant for ages seem to awaken suddenly, under the proper stimuli, and develop into
dynamic powers. In the Fertile Crescent lies the
field of opportunity. A Hammurabi makes his
appearance in Babylon, a Moses in Sinai, a Zenobia in Palmyra, a Philip the Arab in Rome or a
Harun al-Rashid in Baghdad. Monuments are
built, like those of Petra, which still arouse the
admiration of the world. The phenomenal and
almost unparalleled efflorescence of early Islam
was due in no small measure to the latent powers
of the Bedouins, who, in the words of the Caliph
Umar, "furnished Islam with its raw material."

On the Eve of the Rise of Islam

"Island" though it was, the Arabian peninsula did not escape the attentions of the outside world. The first unmistakable reference to the Arabians as such occurs in an inscription of the Assyrian Shalmaneser III, who in 854 B.C. led an expedition against the King of Damascus and his allies, among whom was an Arabian sheikh. It is typical of the spirit and of most of the events of the time: "Karkar, his royal city, I destroyed, I devastated, I burned with fire. 1,200 chariots, 1,200 cavalry, 20,000 soldiers of Hadad-ezer, of Aram [Damascus] . . . 1,000 camels of Gindibu, the Arabian." It is also significant that the first Arabian in recorded history should be associated with the camel.

We have thus far used the term Arabian for all the inhabitants of the peninsula without re-

gard for geographic location. But we must differentiate between the Arabians of the South and
the North, the latter including the Najdis of Central Arabia. The geographical division of the
lands by the trackless desert into northern and
southern sections has its counterpart in the peoples who inhabit it.

The racial affinities of the people of the north
are with the Mediterranean race; those of the
south are with the Alpine type styled Armenoid,
Hittite or Hebrew and characterized by a broad
jaw and aquiline nose, flat cheeks and abundant
hair. The South Arabians were the first to rise to
prominence and to develop a civilization of their
own. The North Arabians did not step onto
the stage of international affairs until the advent
of Islam in medieval times. It is necessary to mark
the distinction, since the gulf between the two
Arabian stocks was never bridged, even after
Islam had apparently unified the Arabian nation.
This had serious effects, later, in weakening the
Arab empire.

Like a thick wedge the Arabian peninsula
thrusts itself between the two earliest seats of culture: Egypt and Babylonia. It could not escape
their influence. Africa touches Arabia in the
north at the Sinai peninsula—the home of Mt.
Sinai of biblical fame. A land route came down
from there; another, the chief one, followed the
Nile and bent near Thebes to the Red Sea. During the Twelfth Egyptian Dynasty, about 2000
B.C., a canal, the antecedent of the Suez, connected the eastern arm of the Nile with the head

of the Red Sea. Restored by the Ptolemies and
again by the caliphs, it was used until the discovery of the route to India around the Cape of
Good Hope in 1497 to 1498. In the south, the
peninsula is separated from Africa by only fifteen
miles of water.

In the pre-Islamic age the Arabians were not a
military people. Their history was that of traders
—of a prosperous maritime civilization in the
south, which linked India with Africa, and in the
north was memorable for the rise of two great
cities on the trade routes, Petra and Palmyra,
both in due course "destroyed," "devastated,"
and both now magnificent and notable ruins.
Petra, which reached its greatest wealth and prosperity under the patronage of the Romans, was a
city carved from solid rock. Palmyra, located in
the Syrian desert between the rival empires of
the Romans and the Parthians, has left us also
the lovely tale of its ruler, the beautiful and ambitious Zenobia, self-styled Queen of the East,
who stretched the frontiers of her kingdom to
include Egypt and a large part of Asia Minor.
When her generals were defeated in battle in 272
by the Emperor Aurelian, she fled from Palmyra
on a swift dromedary into the desert; but the
long arm of Rome caught up with her. She was
honored, in the spirit of the day, by being loaded
with golden chains when led before the victor's
chariot in his triumphal entry into Rome.

A less spectacular episode in the early history
of the peninsula, but one far more deeply significant, was the forty-year sojourn of the Hebrew

tribes in Sinai and the Nufud, on their way to
Palestine from Egypt about 1225 B.C. In Midian,
the southern part of Sinai and the land east of it,
the divine covenant was made. Moses, the leader
of the tribes, there married an Arabian woman,
the daughter of a Midianite priest (Exodus
3:1; 18:10-12), and this union led to one of the
most significant of all events in history. The wife
of Moses was a worshiper of a God named Yahu,
who became Yahweh, or Jehovah. He was a desert God, simple and austere. His abode was a tent
and his ritual not elaborate, consisting chiefly in
desert feasts and sacrifices and burnt offerings
from the herds. The daughter of the Midianite
priest instructed Moses in this cult. What vast
events were to follow!

Echoes of the desert origin of the Hebrews
abound in the Old Testament. The "kings" of
the prophet Jeremiah were in all probability
sheikhs of northern Arabia and the Syrian desert.
The Shunamite damsel whose beauty is immortalized in the Song ascribed to Solomon was probably an Arabian of the Kedar tribe. Job, the author of the finest piece of poetry that the ancient
Semitic world produced, was an Arab, not a Jew.
The "wise men from the East" who followed the
star to Jerusalem were possibly Bedouins from
the North Arabian desert rather than Magi from
Persia. The Jews were geographically the next-
door neighbors of the Arabians and racially their
next of kin. The list of biblical associations could
be infinitely extended.

On the Eve of the Rise of Islam

But it is the rise of Islam, the religion of submission to the will of Allah, which concerns us most here. It is sufficient to note that by the beginning of the seventh century of the Christian era, the national life developed in early South Arabia had become utterly disrupted; anarchy prevailed. Throughout the entire peninsula the antiquated paganism of the Arabians, which, for the Bedouin, centered chiefly on the worship of a moon-god (as is likely to be the case with pastoral people in hot climates who find the coolness of the night their friend and the sun their enemy) had reached a point where it failed any longer to meet the spiritual demands of the people. Vague monotheistic ideas had already appeared and developed into a cult. Christian and Jewish communities were established in Najran, South Arabia. Jewish tribes flourished in Yathrib (later Medina), Hijaz. From Syria and Abyssinia came Christian traders and slaves to the markets of Mecca. Christian influences had been increasingly felt, although the Christian idea had never caught hold of the Arab imagination. But the stage was set and the time had come for the rise of a great religious and national leader.

Moslems call the era before the appearance of Muhammad the Jahiliyah period, a term usually rendered as "time of ignorance" or "barbarism." Although the North Arabians produced no system of writing almost until the time of Muhammad, "barbarism" is too strong a word to apply to the society which had been developed

25

in South Arabia; this was the period in which Arabia had no dispensation, no inspired prophet, no revealed book.

No people in the world have such enthusiastic admiration for literary expression and are so moved by the word, spoken or written, as the Arabs. Hardly any language seems capable of exercising over the minds of its users such irresistible influence as Arabic. Modern audiences in Baghdad, Damascus and Cairo can be stirred to the highest degree by the recital of poems only vaguely comprehended, and by the delivery of orations in the classical tongue, though only partially understood. The rhythm, the rhyme, the music, produce on them the effect of what they call "lawful magic."

Typical Semites, the Arabians created or developed no great art of their own. Their artistic nature found expression chiefly through one medium: speech. If the Greek glorified in his statues and architecture, the Arabian found in his ode, and the Hebrew in his psalm, a finer mode of self-expression. "The beauty of man," declares an Arabic adage, "lies in the eloquence of his tongue." "Wisdom," in a late saying, "has alighted on three things: the brain of the Franks, the hands of the Chinese and the tongue of the Arabs." Eloquence (i.e. ability to express oneself forcefully and elegantly in both prose and poetry), archery and horsemanship were considered in the Jahiliyah period the three basic attributes of "the perfect man." By virtue of its peculiar structure Arabic lent itself admirably to

a terse, epigrammatic manner of speech. Islam
made full use of this feature of the language and
of this psychological peculiarity of its people.
Hence the "miraculous character" of the style
and composition of the Koran, adduced by Moslems as the strongest argument in favor of the
genuineness of their faith. The triumph of Islam
was to a certain extent the triumph of a language,
more particularly of a book.

It was only in the field of poetical expression
that the pre-Islamic Arabian excelled. The Bedouin's love of poetry was his one cultural asset.

As his office developed, the poet acquired a
variety of functions. In battle his tongue was as
effective as his people's bravery. In peace he
might prove a menace to public order by his
fiery harangues. His poem might arouse a tribe
to action in the same manner as the tirade of
a demagogue in a modern political campaign.
As the press agent, the journalist, of his day his
favor was sought by princely gifts. His poems,
committed to memory and transmitted from one
tongue to another, offered an invaluable means
of publicity. He was at the same time the molder
and the agent of public opinion. "Cutting off
the tongue" was the classical expression for sub-
sidizing the poet and thus avoiding his satires.

Besides being oracle, guide, orator and spokes-
man of his community the poet was its historian
and scientist, in so far as it had a scientist.
Bedouins measured intelligence by poetry. "Who
dares dispute my tribe . . . its preeminence in
horsemen, poets and numbers?" exclaims a bard.

In these three elements—military power, intelligence and numbers—lay the superiority of a tribe.

Aside from its poetic interest and the worth of its grace and elegance, ancient poetry, therefore, has historical importance as source material for the study of the period in which it was composed. In fact it is our only quasi-contemporaneous data. It throw light on all phases of pre-Islamic life. Hence the adage, "Poetry is the public register of the Arabians."

Judged by his poetry the pagan Bedouin of the age before Muhammad had little if any religion. His conformity to religious practice followed tribal inertia and was dictated by his conservative respect for tradition. Nowhere do we find an illustration of genuine devotion to a heathen deity. The Bedouin peopled the desert with living things of beastly nature called jinn or demons. These jinn differ from the gods not so much in their nature as in their relation to man. The gods are on the whole friendly; the jinn hostile—personifications of the fantastic notions of the terrors of the desert and its wild animal life. Even after Islam the idea of the jinn persisted; indeed, the number of jinn increased, since the heathen deities were then degraded into such beings.

But in the city of Mecca, in the territory of Hijaz, the barren country standing like a barrier between the uplands of Najd and the low coastal region, there was a deity—not the only deity—named Allah. The name is an ancient one. Allah was held by the people of Mecca to be the creator, the supreme provider, the god to be invoked in time of greatest peril. And soon now, from the lips of a man from this city of Mecca, was to ring out the greatest phrase of the Arabic language, the resonant and electrifying cry which was to drive the people of the desert out of their insularity almost to the limits of the known world: *la ilaha illa-'llah!* There is no god but Allah!

Muhammad,
The Prophet of Allah

In or about A.D. 571 a child was born to the Quraysh, a high-ranking tribe which was custodian of the shrine called Kaaba, a pantheon of multitudinous deities and a center of pilgrimage at Mecca, and was given by his mother a name which may remain forever uncertain. His tribe called him al-Amin (the faithful), apparently an honorific title. The form which his name takes in the Koran is Muhammad, and once Ahmad. The name, which means "highly praised," is borne by more male children than any other in the world. The baby's father died before his birth; the mother when he was about six years old.

Though the only one of the world prophets to be born within the full light of history, Muhammad is but little known to us in his early life:

of his struggle for a livelihood, his efforts toward self-fulfillment and his gradual and painful realization of the great task awaiting him we have but few reliable reports. But with his marriage at the age of twenty-five to the wealthy and high-minded widow Khadijah, fifteen years his senior, Muhammad steps upon the threshold of clear history. Khadijah was a Qurayshite and, as a well-to-do merchant's widow, was conducting business independently and had taken young Muhammad into her employ. As long as this lady with her strong personality and noble character lived, Muhammad would have none other for a wife.

Muhammad now had leisure and was able to pursue his own inclinations. He was then often noticed secluding himself and engaging in meditation in a little cave on a hill outside of Mecca. It was in the course of one of these periods of distraction caused by doubts and yearning after the truth that Muhammad heard a voice commanding: "Recite thou in the name of thy Lord who created" (Koran 96:1). Evidently what was primarily weighing on Muhammad's heart was the observation that the Jews had a book, a revelation, and the Christians had a book and were all progressive and prosperous, whereas the Arabians had no book and were comparatively backward. This was his first revelation. The Prophet had received his call. When after a brief interval following his call to the prophetic office, the second vision came, Muhammad, under the stress of great emotion, rushed home in alarm and asked

31

his wife to put some covers on him, whereupon these words "descended": "O thou, enwrapped in they mantle! Arise and warn" (Koran 74:1). The voices varied and sometimes came like the "reverberating of bells" but later became one voice, identified as that of Gabriel.

The message of the Arabian Muhammad was a parallel of the message of the Hebrew prophets of the Old Testament. God is one. He is all-powerful. He is the creator of the universe. There is a judgment day. Splendid rewards in Paradise await those who carry out God's commands, and terrible punishment in hell for those who disregard them. Such was the gist of his early message.

Consecrated and fired by the new task which he felt called upon to perform as the messenger of Allah, Muhammad now went among his own people teaching, preaching, delivering the new message. They laughed him to scorn. He turned warner, prophet of doom, seeking to effect his purpose by vivid and thrilling descriptions of the joys of Paradise and the terrors of hell, even threatening his hearers with imminent doom. But short, crisp and impressive as were his early revelations, Muhammad was gaining few converts. His wife, his cousin Ali, and his kinsman abu-Bakr acknowledged him, but the aristocratic and influential branch of Quraysh stood adamant. Slowly, however, new recruits, mainly from among the slave and lower classes, began to swell the ranks of the believers. The ridicule and sarcasm which had hitherto been used unsparingly on the part of the Quraysh were no longer deemed effective as weapons; it became necessary to resort to active persecution. These new measures forced the migration to Abyssinia of eleven Meccan families, converts to the new faith, followed in 615 by some eighty-three others. The émigrés found asylum in the domain of the Christian Negus, who was unbending in his refusal to deliver them into the hands of their oppressors. Undaunted through these dark days of persecution by the temporary loss of so many followers, Muhammad fearlessly continued to preach and by persuasion convert men from the worship of the many and false gods to that of the one and true God, Allah. Revelations continued to "descend." He who had marveled at the Jews and Christians having a "scripture" was determined that his people, too, should have one.

Soon Umar ibn-al-Khattab, destined to play a leading role in the establishment of the Islamic state, was enrolled in the service of Allah. Within this period there also falls the dramatic nocturnal journey in which the Prophet is said to have been instantly transported from the Kaaba to Jerusalem preliminary to his ascent to the seventh heaven. Since it thus served as the terrestrial station on this memorable journey, Jerusalem, already sacred to the Jews and Christians, became and has remained the third holiest city after Mecca and Medina in the Moslem world. Embellished by later accretions, the story of this miraculous trip still is a favorite in mystic circles in Persia and Turkey. A Spanish scholar con-

33

siders it the original source of Dante's *Divine Comedy*. That the memory of the journey is still a living, moving force in Islam is illustrated by the serious disturbance in Palestine in August 1929. The trouble centered on the Wailing Wall of the Jews in Jerusalem, which the Moslems consider the halting place of the winged horse with a woman's face and peacock's tail on which Muhammad journeyed heavenward.

Two years after the miraculous journey a deputation of about seventy-five men invited Muhammad to make Medina his home. In that city the Jews, who were looking forward to a Messiah, had evidently prepared their heathen compatriots for such a claimant. Muhammad allowed two hundred followers to elude the vigilance of the Quraysh and slip quietly into Medina, his mother's native city; he himself followed and arrived there on September 24, 622. Such was the famous hegira—not entirely a "flight," but a scheme of migration carefully considered for some two years. Seventeen years later the Caliph Umar designated that lunar year (beginning July 16) in which the hegira took place as the official starting point of the Moslem era.

The hegira, with which the Meccan period ended and the Medinese period began, proved a turning point in the life of Muhammad. Leaving the city of his birth as a despised prophet, he entered the city of his adoption as an honored chief. The seer in him now recedes into the background and the practical man of politics comes

34

to the fore. The prophet is overshadowed by the statesman.

Taking advantage of the periods of "holy truce" and anxious to offer sustenance to the Emigrants, the Medinese Moslems (called Supporters) under the leadership of the new chief intercepted a summer caravan on its return from Syria to Mecca, thus striking at the most vital point in the life of that commercial metropolis. The caravan leader had learned of the scheme and sent to Mecca for aid. The encounter between the reinforced Meccan caravan and the Moslems, thanks to the inspiring leadership of the Prophet, resulted in the complete victory of three hundred Moslems over a thousand Meccans. However unimportant in itself as a military engagement, this skirmish laid the foundation of Muhammad's temporal power. Islam had won its first and decisive military victory: the victory itself was interpreted as a divine sanction of the new faith.

The spirit of discipline and the contempt of death manifested at this first armed encounter of Islam proved characteristic of it in its later and greater conquests. True, in the following year the Meccans avenged their defeat and even wounded the Prophet, but their triumph was not to endure. Islam recovered and passed on gradually from the defensive to the offensive, its propagation now assured. Hitherto it had been a religion within a state; in Medina it passed into something more than a state religion—it became

35

the state. Then and there Islam came to be what the world has ever since recognized it to be—a militant polity.

Muhammad then conducted a campaign against the Jews for "siding with the confederates," which resulted in the killing of six hundred able-bodied men of their leading tribe and the expulsion of the rest. The Emigrants were established on the date plantations thus made ownerless. This tribe was the first but not the last body of Islam's foes to be offered the alternative of apostasy or death.

In this Medinese period the Arabianization, the nationalization, of Islam was effected. The new prophet broke with both Judaism and Christianity; Friday was substituted for Sabbath; the call from the minaret was decreed in place of trumpets and bells; Ramadan was fixed as a month of fasting, the direction to be observed during the ritual prayer was changed from Jerusalem to Mecca, the pilgrimage to the Kaaba was authorized and the kissing of the Black Stone—a pre-Islamic fetish—sanctioned.

In 628 Muhammad led a body of 1,400 believers to the city of his birth and exacted the pact in which Meccans and Moslems were treated on equal terms. This treaty practically ended the conflict between Muhammad and his people, the Quraysh. Among other members of this tribe, Khalid ibn-al-Walid and Amr ibn-al-As, destined to become the two mighty swords of militant Islam, were about this time received as recruits to the great cause. Two years later, toward the end of January 630 (Anno Hegirae 8), the conquest of Mecca was complete. Entering its great sanctuary, Muhammad smashed the many idols, said to have numbered three hundred and sixty, exclaiming: "Truth hath come, and falsehood hath vanished!" The people themselves, however, were treated with special magnanimity. Hardly a triumphal entry in ancient annals is comparable to this.

It was probably about this time that the territory around the Kaaba was declared by Muhammad forbidden and sacred, and the passage of the Koran was revealed which was later interpreted as prohibiting all non-Moslems from approaching it. This verse was evidently intended to forbid only the polytheists from drawing near to the Kaaba at the time of the annual pilgrimage, but the injunction as interpreted is still effective. No more than fifteen Christian-born Europeans have thus far succeeded in seeing the two Holy Cities and escaping with their lives. The first to leave a record was Ludovico di Varthema of Bologna in 1503, and one of the latest was the Englishman, Eldon Rutter. The most interesting was undoubtedly Sir Richard Burton.

In the year A.H. 9 Muhammad concluded treaties of peace with the Christian chief of al-Aqabah and the Jewish tribes in the oases of Maqna, Adhruh and Jarba to the south. The native Jews and Christians were taken under the protection of the newly arising Islamic community in consideration of a payment later called *jizyah*, which included land and head tax. This

37

act set a precedent far-reaching in its future consequences.

This year 9 (630-631) is called the "year of
delegations." During it deputations flocked from
near and far to offer allegiance to the prince-
prophet. Tribes joined out of convenience if not
conviction, and Islam contented itself with ex-
acting a verbal confession of faith and a payment of a tax. Groups came from distant Oman,
Hadramawt and Yaman. The leading tribes sent
deputies. Arabia, which had hitherto never
bowed to the will of one man, seemed now in-
clined to be dominated by Muhammad and to be
incorporated into his new scheme. Its heathen-
ism was yielding to a nobler faith and a higher
morality.

In the tenth Moslem year Muhammad headed
triumphantly the annual pilgrimage into his new
religious capital, Mecca. This proved his last
visit and was styled "the farewell pilgrimage."
Three months after his return to Medina he un-
expectedly took ill and died, complaining of
severe headache, on June 8, 632.

To the Medinese period in the life of the
Prophet belong the lengthy and more verbose
chapters of the Koran which contain, in addition
to the religious laws governing fasting and almsgiving and prayer, social and political ordinances
dealing with marriage and divorce, and the treatment of slaves, prisoners of war and enemies.
The legislation of him who was himself once a
poor orphan is especially benevolent on behalf

of the slave, the orphan, the weak and the oppressed.

Even at the height of his glory Muhammad led, as in his days of obscurity, an unpretentious life in one of those clay houses consisting, as do all old-fashioned houses of present-day Arabia and Syria, of a few rooms opening into a courtyard and accessible only from it. He was often seen mending his own clothes and was at all times within the reach of his people. "Serious or trivial," says Hogarth, "his daily behaviour has instituted a canon which millions observe at this day with conscious mimicry. No one regarded by any section of the human race as Perfect Man has been imitated so minutely."

The little wealth he left he regarded as state property. He took about a dozen wives, some for love, others for political reasons, among all of whom his favorite was Aishah, the young daughter of abu-Bakr. By Khadijah he had a number of children, none of whom survived him except Fatimah, later to be the famous spouse of Ali. Muhammad mourned bitterly the loss of his infant son Ibrahim, born to him by Mary, a Christian Copt.

Out of the religious community of Medina the later and larger state of Islam arose. This new community of Emigrants and Supporters was established on the basis of religion as the Ummah, or congregation of Allah. This was the first attempt in the history of Arabia at a social organization with religion, rather than blood, as its basis. Allah was the personification of state supremacy. His Prophet, as long as he lived, was His legitimate vice-regent and supreme ruler on earth. As such, Muhammad exercised, in addition to his spiritual function, the same temporal authority that any chief of a state might exercise. All persons within this community, regardless of tribal affiliation and older loyalties, were now brethren at least in principle. These are the words of the Prophet in his noble sermon at the "farewell pilgrimage":

"O ye men! harken unto my words and take ye them to heart! Know ye that every Moslem is a brother to every other Moslem, and that ye are now one brotherhood. It is not legitimate for any one of you, therefore, to appropriate unto himself anything that belongs to his brother unless it is willingly given him by that brother."

Thus by one stroke the most vital bond of Arab relationship, that of tribal kinship, was replaced by a new bond, that of faith. Herein lies one of the chief claims of Muhammad to originality. A sort of Pax Islamica was instituted for Arabia. The new community was to have no priesthood, no hierarchy, no central see. Its mosque was its public forum and military drill ground as well as its place of common worship. The leader in prayer, the *imam*, was also to be commander in chief of the army of the faithful, who were enjoined to protect one another against the entire world. All Arabians who remained heathen were outside the pale, almost outlaws. Islam canceled the past. Wine and gambling—

next to women the two indulgences dearest to the Arabian heart—were abolished in one verse. Singing, almost equally attractive, was frowned upon.

From Medina the Islamic theocracy spread all over Arabia and later encompassed the larger part of Western Asia and North Africa. The community of Medina was in miniature the subsequent community of Islam. Within a brief span of mortal life Muhammad called forth out of unpromising material a nation never united before, in a country that was hitherto but a geographical expression; established a religion which in vast areas superseded Christianity and Judaism and still claims the adherence of a goodly portion of the human race; and laid the basis of an empire that was soon to embrace within its far-flung boundaries the fairest provinces of the then civilized world. Himself an unschooled man, Muhammad was nevertheless responsible for a book still considered by one-seventh of mankind as the embodiment of all science, wisdom and theology.

The Book and the Faith

Today the sight of a Moslem picking up a piece of paper from the street and tucking it carefully into a hole in a wall, lest the name of Allah be on it, is not rare. The Koran, the Book of Allah, is treated with unbounded reverence by the Moslem. It is the word of God, dictated through Gabriel to Muhammad. "Let none touch it but the purified" (56:78).

Although there are approximately twice as many Christians as Moslems in the world it can safely be said that the Koran is the most widely read book ever written. For besides its use in worship it is the textbook from which practically every young Moslem learns to read Arabic. Other than the official translation into Turkish there is no authorized Moslem translation; it has, however, been done without authoriza-

42

tion into some forty languages. It is readily available in Rodwell's English translation in Everyman's Library. The first translation was that into Latin, undertaken in the twelfth century by Peter the Venerable, abbot of Cluny, in an attempt to refute the beliefs of Islam and discredit its founder. The first translation into English appeared in 1649, made from the French, by Alexander Ross, Vicar of Carisbrooke: *"The Alcoran of Mohamet . . .* newly Englished, for the satisfaction of all that desire to look into the Turkish vanities."

Compared to the Bible, the Koran offers but few textual uncertainties. The first, final and only canonized version of the Koran was collated nineteen years after the death of Muhammad, when it was seen that the memorizers of the Koran were becoming extinct through the battles that were decimating the ranks of the believers. From passages written on "ribs of palm-leaves and tablets of white stone and from the breasts of men" an earlier but unofficial text had been constructed. All other copies were then destroyed. Its 6,239 verses, its 77,934 words, even its 323,621 letters have since been painstakingly counted. Not all enumerations of its contents, however, yield exactly the same figures. The Book is not only the heart of a religion, the guide to a Kingdom of Heaven, but a compendium of science and a political document, embodying a code of laws for a kingdom on earth.

The parallels between the Old Testament and the Koran are many and striking. Almost all the historical narratives of the Koran have their biblical counterparts. Among the Old Testament characters, Adam, Noah, Abraham (mentioned about seventy times), Ishmael, Lot, Joseph, Moses (whose name occurs in thirty-four chapters), Saul, David, Solomon, Elijah, Job and Jonah figure prominently. The story of the Creation and Fall of Adam is cited five times, the flood eight and Sodom eight. Of the New Testament characters Zacharias, John the Baptist, Jesus and Mary are the only ones emphasized. But many old Semitic proverbs and sayings common to both Hebrew and Arab are found in New or Old Testaments and in the Koran—such, for example, as those dealing with "an eye for an eye," "the house built upon sand," "the camel and the needle's eye," and the "taste of death for every man." Certain miraculous acts attributed to Jesus the Child in the Koran, such as speaking out in the cradle and creating birds out of clay, recall similar acts recorded in the Apocryphal Gospels.

The religion of the Koran comes nearer the Judaism of the Old Testament than does the Christianity of the New Testament. It has such close affinities with both, however, that in its early stages it must have appeared more like a heretic Christian sect than a distinct religion. In his *Divine Comedy* Dante consigns Muhammad to one of the lower hells with "sowers of scandals and schism."

The arrangement of the chapters (termed *surahs* in Arabic) is mechanical, in the order of their length. The early ones, written in Mecca,

about ninety in number and belonging to the
period of struggle, are mostly short, incisive,
fiery, impassioned in style and replete with prophetic feeling. In them the oneness of Allah, His
attributes, the ethical duties of man and the coming retribution are the favorite themes. The
Medinese surahs, the remaining twenty-four
(about one-third of the contents of the Koran)
which "were sent down" in the period of victory, are mostly long, verbose and rich in legisla-
tive material. In them theological dogmas and
ceremonial regulations relating to the institution
of public prayer, fasting, pilgrimage and the
sacred months are laid down. They contain laws
prohibiting wine, pork and gambling; fiscal and
military ordinances relating to almsgiving and
holy war (the famous *jihad* of the Moslems);
civil and criminal laws regarding homicide, re-
taliation, theft, usury, marriage and divorce,
adultery, inheritance and the freeing of slaves.
The often-quoted prescription for marriage
limits rather than introduces the practice of
polygamy. Critics consider the statutes relating
to divorce (4:24, 33:48, 2:229) the most objectionable, and those about the treatment of slaves,
orphans and strangers (4:2, 3, 40; 16:73; 24:33)
the most humane portions of Islamic legislation.
The freeing of slaves is encouraged as something
most pleasing to God and an expiation for many
a sin.

The word Koran (*Qur'an*) itself means recitation, lecture, discourse. This book, a strong, living voice, is meant for oral recitation and should

be heard in the original to be appreciated. No small measure of its force lies in its rhyme and rhetoric and in its cadence and sweep, which cannot be reproduced when the book is translated. Its length is four-fifths that of the New Testament in Arabic. The religious influence it exercises as the basis of Islam and the final authority in matters spiritual and ethical are only part of the story. Theology, jurisprudence and science being considered by Moslems as different aspects of one and the same thing, the Koran becomes the scientific manual, the textbook, for acquiring a liberal education. In such an institution as al-Azhar, the largest Moslem university in the world, this book still holds its own as the basis of the whole curriculum. Its literary influence may be appreciated when we realize that it was due to it alone that the various dialects of the Arabic-speaking peoples have not developed into distinct languages, as have the Romance languages. While today an Iraqi may find it a little difficult fully to understand the speech of a Moroccan, he would have no difficulty in understanding his written language, since in both Iraq and Morocco—as well as in Syria, Arabia, Egypt —the classical language modeled by the Koran is followed closely everywhere. At the time of Muhammad there was no work of the first order in Arabic prose. The Koran was therefore the earliest, and has ever since remained the model prose work. Its language is rhythmical and rhetorical, but not poetical. Its rhymed prose has set the standard which almost every conserva-

tive Arabic writer of today consciously strives
to imitate.

In his *Literary History of the Arabs*, Nichol-
son tries to preserve some of the Arabic flavor
in the opening *surah* by translating it thus:

> In the name of God, the merciful, who for-
> giveth aye!
> Praise to God, the Lord of all that be,
> The merciful, who forgiveth aye,
> The King of Judgment Day!
> Thee we worship and for Thine aid we pray.
> Lead us in the right way,
> The way of those to whom Thou hast been
> gracious, against whom Thou hast not
> waxed wroth, and who go not astray!

In dealing with the fundamentals of their religion Moslem theologians distinguish between
religious belief and acts of worship, or religious
duty.

Religious belief, *iman*, involves belief in
God and in His angels, His "books" and His mes-
sengers and in the last day. Its first and greatest
dogma is: *la ilaha illa-'llah*, no god but Allah. In
iman the conception of God stands supreme. In
fact, over ninety per cent of Moslem theology
has to do with Allah. He is the one true God, the
supreme reality, the pre-existent, the creator,
the omniscient, the omnipotent, the self-subsist-
ent. He has ninety-nine names and as many attributes. The full Moslem rosary has ninety-nine
beads corresponding to His names. His attributes

of love are overshadowed by those of might and majesty. Islam is the religion of "submission," "surrender," to the will of Allah. The submission of Abraham and his son in the supreme test, the attempted sacrifice by the father, expressed in the verb *aslama* (37:103), was evidently the act that provided Muhammad with the name for the new faith. In this uncompromising monotheism, with its simple, enthusiastic faith in the supreme rule of a transcendent being, lies the chief strength of Islam as a religion. Its adherents enjoy a contentment and resignation unknown among followers of other creeds. Suicide is rare in Moslem lands.

The second dogma in *iman* treats of Muhammad as the messenger (*rasul*) of Allah, His prophet, the admonisher of his people, the last of a long line of prophets of whom he is the "seal," and therefore the greatest. In the koranic system of theology Muhammad is but a human being whose only miracle is the elegance of the composition of the Koran; but in tradition, folklore and popular belief he is invested with a divine aura. His religion is preeminently a practical one, reflecting the practical and efficient mind of its originator. It offers no unattainable ideal, few theological complications and perplexities, no mystical sacraments and no priestly hierarchy involving ordination, consecration and "apostolic succession."

The Koran is the word of Allah. It contains the final revelation, and is "uncreated." A koranic quotation is always introduced with "saith

The Book and the Faith

Allah." In its phonetic and graphic reproduction and in its linguistic form the Koran is identical and coeternal with a heavenly archetype. Of all miracles it is the greatest: all men and jinn in collaboration could not produce its like.

In its angelology Islam gives the foremost place to Gabriel, the bearer of revelation, who is also "the spirit of holiness" and "the faithful spirit." As a messenger of the supreme deity he corresponds to the Hermes of Greek mythology.

Sin can be either moral or ceremonial. The worst and only unpardonable sin is *shirk*, joining or associating other gods with the one true God. Ascribing plurality to the Deity seemed most detestable to Muhammad, and in the Medinese surahs the polytheists are continually threatened with the last judgment. In Muhammad's mind "the people of the book," the Scripturaries, i.e. the Christians and Jews, were probably not included among the polytheists, though some commentators would hold a different view.

The most impressive parts of the Koran deal with the future life. The reality of future life is emphasized by the recurrent references to "the day of judgment," "the day of resurrection," "the day," "the hour" and "the inevitable." Future life as depicted in the Koran, with its bodily pains and physical pleasures, implies the resurrection of the body.

The acts of worship, or religious duties, of the Moslem center on the so-called five pillars of Islam.

The profession of faith, which is the first pil-

49

The Arabs

lar, is summed up in the tremendous formula *la ilaha illa-'llah: Muhammadun rasulu-'llah* (No god but Allah: Muhammad is the messenger of Allah). These are the first words to strike the ear of the new-born Moslem babe; they are the last to be uttered at the grave. And between birth and death no other words are more often repeated. They occur in the muezzin's call to prayer, chanted many times daily from the tops of minarets. Islam has generally satisfied itself with only a verbal profession; once the formula is accepted and reproduced the person is nominally a Moslem.

Five times a day—dawn, midday, midafternoon, sunset and nightfall—is the faithful Moslem supposed to turn his face toward Mecca and recite his prescribed prayer. Prayer is the second pillar of faith. A bird's-eye view of the Moslem world at the hour of prayer would present the spectacle of a series of concentric circles of worshipers radiating from the Kaaba at Mecca and covering an ever-widening area from Sierra Leone to Canton and from Tobolsk to Cape Town.

The ritual prayer is a legally defined act performed by all with the same general bodily postures and genuflections and with the same proper orientation. The worshiper should be in a state of legal purity, and the use of Arabic as a medium of expression is absolutely incumbent upon him, no matter what his native tongue may be. In its stereotyped form prayer is not so much petition or supplication as it is the mention of Allah's name. The simple and meaningful *fatihah* or opening surah, often likened to the Lord's Prayer, is reiterated by the faithful Moslem about twenty times a day, one of the most often repeated formulas ever devised. Doubly meritorious is the voluntary ritual prayer performed at night, for it is a work of supererogation.

The Friday noon prayer is the only public one and is obligatory for all adult males. Certain mosques have places reserved for women. One feature of the Friday service is the sermon delivered by the leader (*imam*), in which intercessory prayer is offered on behalf of the ruling head of the state. This congregational assembly had for its prototype the Jewish synagogue worship, but was influenced in its later development by the Christian Sunday service. In dignity, simplicity and orderliness it is unsurpassed as a form of collective worship. Standing erect in self-arranged rows in the mosque and following the leadership of the *imam* with precision and reverence, the worshipers present a sight that is always impressive. As a disciplinary measure this congregational prayer must have had great value for the proud, individualistic sons of the desert, developing in them a sense of social equality and a consciousness of solidarity. It promoted that brotherhood of believers which the religion of Muhammad had theoretically substituted for blood relationship. The prayer ground became "the first drill ground of Islam."

Prescribed originally as a voluntary act of love and considered almost identical with piety, legal almsgiving constitutes the third pillar of the faith. It evolved into an obligatory tax on property, including money, cattle, corn, fruit and merchandise. The young Islamic state collected it through regular officials and administered it from a central treasury to support the poor among the community, build mosques and defray government expenses. Its underlying principle is something like that of the tithe, which, according to Pliny, the South Arabian merchants had to pay to their god before they were allowed to sell their spices. Its exact amount varied, but generally it averaged two and a half per cent. Even soldiers' pensions were not exempt. Later, with the disintegration of the purely Islamic state, it was again left to the Moslem's conscience.

Though penitential fasts are prescribed a number of times in the Koran, Ramadan as a fasting month is mentioned only once. Abstinence from all food and drink is enjoined from dawn till sunset during Ramadan. Instances in which violence has been used by the government or by the populace against a nonfasting believer in Moslem lands are not unknown. We have no evidence of any practice of fasting in pre-Islamic pagan Arabia, but the institution was, of course, well established among both Christians and Jews and became the fourth pillar of Islam.

Pilgrimage is the fifth and last pillar. Once in a lifetime every Moslem of either sex who can afford it is supposed to undertake at a stated time of the year a holy visit to Mecca. As long as he is in a sanctified state, symbolized by the wearing of a seamless garment, the pilgrim must observe, in addition to the abstinences imposed in connection with the fasting of Ramadan—such as abstinence from sexual intercourse—those special regulations forbidding the shedding of blood, hunting and the uprooting of plants. Pilgrimage to holy places was an ancient Semitic institution echoes of which survived to Old Testament days. Originally it may have been a feature of a solar cult the ceremonies of which coincided with the autumnal equinox and constituted a kind of farewell to the harsh rule of the burning sun and a welcoming to the thunder-god of fertility.

A constant trek of pilgrims across Central Africa, from Senegal, Liberia, Nigeria, is ever on the move eastward and increasing in numbers as it goes along. Some are on foot, others on camel-back. The majority are men, but a few are women and children. They trade, they beg, many fall by the wayside and are martyrs; those who survive finally strike a western Red Sea port whence they are transported across by dhows. But the four major caravans are those from Yaman, Iraq, Syria and Egypt. Each of these countries used to send annually at the head of its caravan a *mahmil* symbolic of its dignity, a splendidly decorated litter, carried on a camel that was led and not ridden. After the conquest of Hijaz (1924) by ibn-Saud at the head of the Wahhabis, this "heathen" rite was abolished.

The average number of pilgrims annually be-

tween the years of the first and second World
Wars was approximately 172,000. However, in
recent years the number has been on the increase,
having already reached the million mark, with
the countries of Egypt, Pakistan and Indonesia
registering the largest number. Down through
the ages this institution has continued to serve
as the major unifying influence in Islam and the
most effective common bond among the diverse
believers. It rendered almost every capable Moslem perforce a traveler for once in his lifetime.
The socializing influence of such a gathering of
the brotherhood of believers from the four quarters of the earth is hard to overestimate. It af-
forded opportunity for Negroes, Berbers, Chinese, Persians, Syrians, Turks, Arabs—rich and
poor, high and low—to fraternize and meet together on the common ground of faith. Of all
world religions Islam seems to have attained the
largest measure of success in demolishing the barriers of race, color and nationality—at least
within the confines of its own community. The
line is drawn only between believers and the
rest of mankind. These gatherings have undoubtedly contributed an important share toward the achievement of that result. They have
further provided excellent opportunities for the
propagation of sectarian ideas among peoples
coming from lands not bound together by the
modern means of communication and where the
press is not yet a living voice.

The duty of *jihad*, holy war, has been raised
to the dignity of a sixth pillar by at least one Mos-

lem sect, the Kharijites. To it Islam owes its unparalleled expansion as a worldly power. It is one of the principal duties of the caliph to keep pushing back the geographical wall separating "the land of Islam" from "the territory of war." Of more recent years, however, *jihad* has found less support in the Moslem world. Islam as late as the second World War flourished under many alien governments considered too strong or benevolent to be overthrown. The last call to a universal uprising against non-Moslems, made in the fall of 1914 by the Ottoman Sultan-Caliph Muhammad Rashad, proved an utter failure. It was made by an Orientalist the subject of a book: *The Holy War Made in Germany*.

Another important article of faith is the decree of good and evil (9:51; 3:139; 35:2), a dominant factor in Moslem thought and conduct through the ages. Whatever happens in this life—be it good or bad—proceeds entirely from the divine will and has been irrevocably decreed. Predestination is a source of great strength in Islam; it is also one of its main weaknesses.

These religious obligations constitute the fundamentals of Islam. They are not the only ones instituted by koranic prescription. Basically there is but one criterion for the conduct of a believer: the will of Allah, as revealed through Muhammad in the Book.

Islam on the March

The two cardinal events of early medieval times are the Teutonic migrations resulting in the disruption of the venerable Roman empire, and the Arab conquests which demolished the Persian empire and shook the Byzantine power to its very foundation. If someone in the first third of the seventh Christian century had had the audacity to prophesy that within a decade or so some unheralded, unforeseen power from the hitherto barbarous and little-known land of Arabia was to make its appearance, hurl itself against the only two world powers of the age, fall heir to the one (the Sasanid) and strip the other (the Byzantine) of its fairest provinces, he would undoubtedly have been declared a lunatic. Yet that was exactly what happened. After the death of the Prophet, sterile Arabia seems to have been converted as if by magic into a nursery of heroes the like of whom, both in number and quality, would be hard to find anywhere. The military campaigns of Khalid ibn-al-Walid and Amr ibn-al-As which ensued in Iraq, Syria, and Egypt are among the most brilliantly executed in the history of warfare and bear favorable comparison with those of Napoleon, Hannibal or Alexander.

The enfeebled condition of the rival Byzantines and Sasanids, who had conducted incessant wars against each other for many generations; the heavy taxes, consequent upon these wars, imposed on the citizens of both empires and undermining their sense of loyalty; the previous domestication of Arabian tribes in Syria and Mesopotamia, particularly along the borders; the existence of schisms in the Christian church, together with the persecution by the orthodox church—all these paved the way for the surprisingly rapid progress of Arabian arms. The native Semites of Syria and Palestine, as well as their Hamite cousins of Egypt, looked upon the Arabian newcomers as nearer of kin than their hated and oppressive alien overlords. In fact the Moslem conquests may be looked upon as the recovery by the ancient Near East of its early domain. Under the stimulus of Islam the East awoke and reasserted itself after a millennium of Western domination. Moreover, the tribute exacted by the new conquerors was less than that exacted by the old, and the conquered could now pursue their religious practices with more freedom. As for the Arabians themselves, they represented

57

The Arabs

a fresh and vigorous stock fired with new enthu-
siasm, imbued with the will to conquer and em-
boldened by the utter contempt of death in-
culcated by their new faith.

But no small share of their seemingly miraculous success was due to their application of a military technique adapted to the open steppes of
Western Asia and North Africa—the use of cavalry and camelry—which the Romans never mas-
tered. The army was divided into center, two
wings, vanguard and rear guard. The cavalry
covered the wings. In the division the tribal unit
was preserved. Each tribe had its own standard,
a cloth attached to a lance, borne by one of the
bravest. The Prophet's banner is said to have
been the eagle. The infantry used bow and arrow, sling and sometimes shield and sword; the
sword was carried in a scabbard flung over the
right shoulder. The javelin was introduced
later from Abyssinia. The chief weapon of the
cavalry was the lance. This, together with the
bow and arrow, formed the two national weapons. The defensive armor, which was lighter than
the Byzantine, was the coat of mail and the
shield.

The order of battle was primitive, in lines or
rows and in compact array. Hostilities began
with individual combats of distinguished champions who stepped forward out of the ranks and
delivered a challenge. The Arabian warrior received higher remuneration than his Persian or
Byzantine rival and was sure of a portion of the
booty. Soldiering was not only the noblest and

most pleasing profession in the sight of Allah but
also the most profitable. The strength of the Moslem Arabian army lay neither in the superiority
of its arms nor in the excellence of its organization but in its higher morale, to which religion
undoubtedly contributed its share; in its power
of endurance, which the desert breeding fostered; and in its remarkable mobility, due mainly
to camel transport.

The "clerical" interpretation of the Islamic
movement, emphasized in Arabic sources, makes
it entirely or primarily a religious movement and
lays no stress on the underlying economic
causes. The corresponding and equally discredited hypothesis held by many Christians
represents the Arabian Moslems as offering the
Koran with one hand and the sword with the
other. Outside of the Arabian peninsula and especially in the instance of the Christians and Jews
there was a third and, from the standpoint of
the conquerors, more desirable choice besides
the Koran and the sword—tribute. "Make war
. . . upon such of those to whom the Book has
been given until they pay tribute offered on the
back of their hands, in a state of humiliation"
(9:29). Islam did provide a new battle-cry, a
convenient rallying point and a party watch-
word. It undoubtedly acted as a cohesive agency
for masses never before united, and furnished a
large part of the driving force. But it is hardly in
itself enough to explain the conquests. Not fanaticism but economic necessity drove the
Bedouin hordes (and most of the armies of con-

quest were recruited from the Bedouins) beyond
the confines of their arid abode to the fair lands
of the north. The dream of heaven in the next
life may have influenced some, but desire for the
comforts and luxuries of the civilized regions of
the Fertile Crescent was just as strong in the case
of many. The Islamic expansion marks the final
stage in the age-long process of gradual infiltration from the barren desert to the adjacent Fertile Crescent, the last great Semitic migration.

The chroniclers, all of whom viewed the
events of the conquest in the light of their subsequent development, would also have us believe
that these campaigns were conducted through
the sagacity of the first caliphs, particularly abu-
Bakr and Umar, in accordance with carefully
prearranged plans. History shows very few cases
in which the course of great events was foreseen
by those who launched them. Far from being entirely the result of deliberate and cool calculation,
the campaigns seem to have started as raids to
provide new outlets for the warring spirit of the
tribes now forbidden to engage in fratricidal
combats, the objective in most cases being booty
and not the gaining of a permanent foothold. But
the machine so built soon got beyond the control
of those who built it. The movement acquired
momentum as the warriors passed from victory
to victory. It was then that the systematic campaigns began, and the creation of the Arab empire followed inevitably. Its creation was therefore due less to early design than to the logic of
immediate circumstances.

The clerical or theological view favoring a providential interpretation of Islamic expansion, corresponding to the Old Testament interpretation of the Hebrew history and to the medieval philosophy of Christian history, has a faulty philological basis. The term Islam may be used in three senses: originally a religion, Islam later became a state, and finally a culture. Unlike Judaism and Buddhism, the religion of Islam proved as much an aggressive and missionary religion as Christianity. Subsequently it built up a state. The Islam that conquered the northern regions was not the Islamic religion but the Islamic state. The Arabians burst forth upon an unsuspecting world as members of a national theocracy. It was Arabianism and not Muhammadanism that triumphed first. Not until the second and third centuries of the Moslem era did the bulk of the people in Syria, Mesopotamia and Persia profess the religion of Muhammad. Between the military conquest of these regions and their religious conversion a long period intervened. And when they were converted the people turned primarily because of self-interest—to escape tribute and seek identification with the ruling class. As for Islam as a culture, it developed slowly after the military conquests on a substratum composed of the heritage of the Syro-Aramaean, Persian and Hellenistic civilizations which had preceded it. With Islam the Near Orient not only recaptured the whole of its former political domain but regained in the realm of culture its ancient intellectual preeminence.

61

The Arabs

But before Arabia could conquer other lands it had first to unify itself. And in the process of seeking that unity it met at once the vexing problem of the successorship to Muhammad, the caliphate.

As long as Muhammad lived he performed the functions of prophet, lawgiver, religious leader, chief judge, commander of the army and civil head of the state—all in one. But now Muhammad was dead. Who was to be his successor, his *khalifah*, or caliph, in all except the spiritual function? In his role as prophet who had delivered the final dispensation to mankind Muhammad could, of course, have no one to succeed him.

The Prophet left no male children. Only one daughter, Fatimah, the wife of Ali, survived him. But the Arabian chiefdom or sheikhdom was not exactly hereditary; it was more electoral, following the line of tribal seniority. So even if his sons had not predeceased him, the problem would not have been solved. Nor did Muhammad clearly designate a successor. The caliphate is the oldest problem Islam has had to face. It is still a living issue. In March 1924, sixteen months after canceling the sultanate, the Kemalist Turks abolished the Ottoman caliphate in Constantinople held by Abd-al-Majid II, and since then a number of pan-Islamic congresses have met in Cairo and Mecca to determine the rightful successor to the Prophet. But all to no avail. "Never was there an Islamic issue which brought about more bloodshed than the caliphate."

62

As always happens when a serious question is thrown open for popular decision, a number of conflicting parties arose after the death of Muhammad. These were, on one side, the Emigrants, who based their claim on having belonged to the tribe of the Prophet and on having been the first to accept his mission. On the other stood the Medinese supporters, who argued that had they not given Muhammad and nascent Islam asylum both would have perished. Later these two parties coalesced to form the Companions. Then came the Legitimists, who reasoned that Allah and Muhammad could not have left the community of believers to the chances and whims of an electorate, and therefore must have made clear provision for its leadership by designating some particular person to succeed Muhammad. Ali, the paternal cousin of the Prophet, the husband of his only surviving daughter and one of the first two or three believers, was the one thus designated as the only legitimate successor. As against the elective principle, this last party held to the divine right of rule. And last the aristocracy of Quraysh, the Umayyads, who held the reins of authority, power and wealth in the pre-Islamic days (but who were the last to profess Islam), asserted their right to the successorship.

The first party triumphed. The aged and pious abu-Bakr, a father-in-law of the Prophet and one of the first three or four to believe in him, received the oath of allegiance from the assembled chiefs. Abu-Bakr headed the list of the four orthodox caliphs, including Umar, Uthman and Ali. This was a period in which the luster of the Prophet's life had not ceased to shed its light and influence over the thoughts and acts of the caliphs. All four were close associates and relatives of the Prophet. The new capital was Medina.

Arab chroniclers say that as soon as Muhammad died all Arabia outside of Hijaz broke off from the newly organized state. The fact is that, with the lack of communication, the utter absence of organized methods of missionary activity and the short time involved, not more than one-third of the peninsula could actually have professed Islam during the life of the Prophet or recognized his rule. Even Hijaz, the immediate scene of his activity, was not Islamized until a year or two before his death.

In a series of short but sharp battles, abu-Bakr conquered the seceders, one after the other, his commander Khalid ibn-al-Walid displaying his talent for generalship. Islam was presently united and ready to march.

Syria, to the north of the peninsula, came first. The Byzantines held it as a part of their heritage from the Romans and Alexander almost a thousand years before. Their generals did not guess that the marauders from Arabia who now began to break across the borders farther than usual were more than casual raiders. They quickly discovered that their foe had a new vigor and with it a fresh weapon—superior mobility. The Arabian camel was bringing a new and irresistible element into warfare. Ordered to go to the relief of Arab troops which were being overpowered by the Byzantines, Khalid, "the sword of Allah," struck by forced camel marches from lower Iraq straight across the trackless desert with a body of veteran fighters and appeared with dramatic suddenness in the neighborhood of Damascus, the Syrian capital. Water for the troops was carried in bags, but for the horses the paunches of the old camels, which were slaughtered for food, served as reservoirs. Two weeks later, with all Arab forces united under his command, Khalid stood before the gate of the city.

Damascus, from whose walls Paul was let down in a basket on the memorable night of his flight, was reputed by tradition to be the oldest city in the world. Soon it was to be the capital of the Islamic empire. It surrendered now, after a six months' siege. Other towns fell like ninepins before the conquerors. There was one more battle. Heraclius, ruler of the Eastern Empire, sent an army of 50,000 men to meet the Moslems. Khalid confronted them with half that number at the valley of the Yarmuk, a tributary of the Jordan, on August 20, 636, a hot day clouded by the windblown dust of one of the most torrid spots on earth. Arab generalship had apparently picked the day with shrewdness. Before the terrific onslaught of the sons of the desert the efforts of the Byzantine troops were of no avail, in spite of the chants and prayers of their priests and the presence of their crosses. The rout of the Byzantines became a slaughter. No further re-

sistance stood in the way of the Arabian arms
until the natural limits of Syria, the Taurus
Mountains, were reached.

So swift and easy an acquisition of so strategic
a territory from the first potentate of the age
gave the newly rising power of Islam prestige in
the eyes of the world and, what is more important, confidence in its own destiny. With Syria as
a base the onward push to Armenia, northern
Mesopotamia, Georgia and Adharbayjan became
possible, as did the raids and attacks which for
many years to come were to be carried on against
Asia Minor.

The same dash and the same tactics again
brought success to the warriors of Allah when
they turned, next, against the Persians. In the
year 637 a great Sasanid army dissolved in panic
on a day of dust storms, and all the fertile low-
lands of Iraq west of the Tigris lay open to the
invaders. With characteristic energy the Moslems
pushed ahead and at a convenient ford effected
a crossing of the Tigris, much swollen by the
spring floods, a feat accomplished without loss
of life to the army. The people of Iraq, like the
people of Syria, welcomed the invaders. Both
Iraqis and Syrians had looked upon their old
masters as an alien and hated power, and neither
the Greek nor the Persian culture, imposed from
the top, had ever been fully assimilated by the
native peoples. The Persian emperor and his
troops deserted their capital, Ctesiphon, without
a fight, and the Moslems entered the greatest
royal city in hither Asia in triumph. With the

death of the emperor, by the hand of one of his subjects who coveted the crown jewels, the last ruler of an empire that had flourished for some twelve centuries passed away—an empire that was not to rise again for some eight centuries.

For the first time, now, the sons of barren Arabia came into direct contact with luxuries and comforts. The royal palace with its spacious audience chamber, graceful arches and sumptuous furnishings and decorations presented a sharp contrast to the mud houses of the peninsula. The education of the Arabians was beginning; and as is often in such cases, not without its humorous mishaps. Camphor, never seen before, was taken for salt and used in cooking. Some warriors hastened to exchange gold, which was unfamiliar, for silver, which was familiar. One soldier, when chided for selling a nobleman's daughter who fell as his share of booty for only 1,000 dirhams, replied that he "never thought there was a number above ten hundred."

Once beyond the boundary of Iraq and into Persia proper, the invaders found stiffening resistance and about a decade was needed to complete the conquest. The Persians were Aryans, not Semites, and presented a well organized military power that had been measuring swords with the Romans for more than four hundred years. But it, too, was totally subdued. The year 643 brought the Arabs to the borders of India.

While this triumphant march was in progress in the east, the Moslem wave was likewise flood-

ing toward the west. The strategic position of
Egypt, lying so dangerously close to both Syria
and Hijaz; the richness of its soil, which made
the land the granary of Constantinople; the fact
that its capital Alexandria was the base of the
Byzantine navy and that the country was the
door to the rest of the North African corridor—
all these considerations caused Arabian eyes to
turn covetously toward the valley of the Nile
quite early in the era of expansion. Seeking to
outshine his illustrious rival Khalid, in 639 Amr
ibn-al-As with 4,000 riders took the beaten track
from Palestine along the coast trod by Abraham,
Cambyses, Alexander, Antiochus, the Holy Family—and later Napoleon and Allenby. It was the
international highway of the ancient world.

Again the story was the same—a rout, a siege
and the cry of victory: *Allahu akbar.* God is
most great! This time Babylon of Egypt had
fallen.

With fresh recruits from Arabia swelling his
army to about 20,000, Amr found himself one
morning gazing at the seemingly impregnable
line of walls and towers guarding Egypt's capital and leading port, Alexandria. On one side rose
the lofty Serapeum, which once housed the temple of Serapis and the great library of Alexandria;
on the other loomed the beautiful cathedral of
St. Mark, once the Caesarian temple begun by
Cleopatra in honor of Julius Caesar and finished
by Augustus; farther west stood the two red
Uswan-granite needles ascribed to Cleopatra,
but in reality the work of Thutmose III (ca. 1450

B.C.), the same two which now adorn the Thames Embankment in London and Central Park in New York; and in the background towered the Pharos, flashing the sun's rays by day and its own fire by night and rightly considered one of the seven wonders of the world. No doubt to the desert Arabians the impression of such a sight must have been not unlike that which the sky-line of modern New York, with its towering skyscrapers, makes upon the immigrant.

Alexandria boasted a garrison of some 50,000. Behind it lay the whole strength of the Byzantine navy, of which the city was the base. The invaders, far inferior in number and in equipment, had not a single ship, no siege machines and no immediate source of supply for their man power.

It was about a year later that the glad tidings were sent to Umar, now caliph in Medina, in the following words: "I have captured a city from the description of which I shall refrain. Suffice it to say that I have seized therein 4,000 villas with 4,000 baths, 40,000 poll-tax paying Jews and four hundred places of entertainment for the royalty." The caliph entertained his general's messenger with bread and dates and held in the Prophet's Mosque a simple but dignified service of thanksgiving. *God is most great.*

The site on which Amr pitched his camp near Babylon became the new capital, al-Fustat, which has survived as Old Cairo. In it the conqueror of Egypt erected a simple mosque, the first to rise in that land, which has survived in its repaired form to this day.

The Arabs

The story that by the caliph's order Amr for six long months fed the numerous bath furnaces of the city with the volumes of the Alexandrian library is, incidentally, one of those tales that make good fiction but bad history. The great Ptolemaic Library was burned as early as 48 B.C. by Julius Caesar. A later one, referred to as the Daughter Library, was destroyed about A.D. 389 as a result of an edict by the Roman Emperor Theodosius. At the time of the Arab conquest, therefore, no library of importance existed in Alexandria and no contemporary writer ever brought the charge against Amr or Umar.

The fall of Egypt left the Byzantine provinces bordering on its west defenseless. After the fall of Alexandria and in order to protect his rear, Amr, with characteristic swiftness, pushed westward at the head of his cavalry. The drive carried the banner of the Prophet along the coast of North Africa to the land of the Berbers in Tripoli. It was soon to go much farther.

The Caliphate

One of the favorite themes of history is the story of young, uncultured people who overcome with their fresh strength an old civilization, only to be fascinated and ultimately weakened by the delights of the new culture to which they are exposed. This theme enters now in the story of the men from Arabia.

By the conquest of the Fertile Crescent and the lands of Persia and Egypt the Arabians came into possession of the earliest seats of civilization in the whole world. In art and architecture, in philosophy, in medicine, in science and literature, in government the original Arabians had nothing to teach and everything to learn. And what voracious appetites they proved to have! With sharp curiosity and latent potentialities never aroused before, these Moslem Arabians in col-

71

laboration with and by the help of their subject peoples began now to assimilate, adapt and reproduce their intellectual and esthetic heritage. In Ctesiphon, Damascus, Jerusalem and Alexandria they viewed, admired and copied the work of the architect, the artisan, the jeweler and the manufacturer. To all these centers of ancient culture they came, they saw—and were conquered.

What we now call "Arab civilization" was Arabian neither in its origins and fundamental structure nor in its principal ethnic aspects. The purely Arabian contribution was in the linguistic and to a certain extent in the religious fields. Throughout the whole period of the caliphate the Syrians, the Persians, the Egyptians and others, as Moslem converts or as Christians and Jews, were the foremost bearers of the torch of enlightenment and learning, just as the subjugated Greeks were in their relation to the victorious Romans. The Arab Islamic civilization was at bottom the Hellenized Aramaic and the Iranian civilization as developed under the aegis of the caliphate and expressed through the medium of the Arabic tongue. In another sense it was the logical continuation of the early Semitic civilization of the Fertile Crescent originated and developed by the Assyro-Babylonians, Phoenicians, Aramaeans and Hebrews. In it the unity of the Mediterranean civilization of Western Asia found its final culmination.

In the first two caliphs, abu-Bakr, who ruled from 632 to 634, and Umar (634-644), we have a clear picture of the kind of man whom Moslem

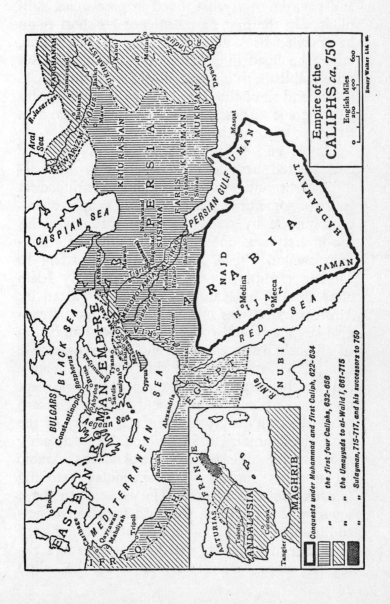

Empire of the CALIPHS ca. 750

English Miles
0 200 400 600

Emery Walker Ltd. sc.

Conquests under Muhammad and first Caliph, 622–634
"   "   the First Four Caliphs, 632–656
"   "   the Umayyads to al-Walid I, 661–715
"   "   Sulayman, 715–717, and his successors to 750

Arabia produced. Abu-Bakr, the conqueror
and pacifier of Arabia, lived in patriarchal simplicity. In the first six months of his short reign
he traveled back and forth daily from al-Sunh,
where he lived in a modest household with his
wife Habibah, to his capital Medina and received
no stipend since the state had at that time hardly
any income. All state business he transacted in
the courtyard of the Prophet's Mosque.

Simple and frugal in manner, his energetic
and talented successor, Umar, who was of towering height and strong physique, continued at
least for some time after becoming caliph to support himself by trade. He lived throughout his
life in a style as unostentatious as that of a Bedouin sheikh. Umar, whose name according to
Moslem tradition is the greatest in early Islam
after that of Muhammad, has been idolized by
Moslem writers for his piety, justice and patriarchal simplicity and treated as the personification
of all the virtues a caliph ought to possess. He
owned, we are told, one shirt and one mantle
only, both conspicuous for their patchwork, slept
on a bed of palm leaves, and had no concern
other than the maintenance of the purity of the
faith, the upholding of justice and the ascendancy
and security of Islam and the Arabians. Arabic
literature is replete with anecdotes extolling
Umar's stern character. He is said to have
scourged his own son to death for drunkenness
and immorality. Having in a fit of anger inflicted
a number of stripes on a Bedouin who came seeking his succor against an oppressor, the caliph

soon repented and asked the Bedouin to inflict the same number on him. But the latter refused. So Umar retired to his home with the following soliloquy:

"O son of al-Khattab! humble thou wert and Allah hath elevated thee; astray, and Allah hath guided thee; weak, and Allah hath strengthened thee. Then He caused thee to rule over the necks of thy people, and when one of them came seeking thy aid, thou didst strike him! What wilt thou have to say to thy Lord when thou presentest thyself before Him?"

It is significant that Umar died, at the zenith of his life, by the poisoned dagger of a Christian Persian slave.

Umar's successor Uthman ruled twelve years and was struck down by Moslems during an uprising. Ali (656-661), next to reign, was acknowledged by practically the entire Moslem world, yet a party soon formed against him and the dynastic wars that were to convulse Islam from time to time and occasionally shake it to its foundation had begun. Five years later Ali was cut down with a poisoned saber.

We should here guard against the common fallacy that the caliphate was a religious office. In this regard analogies drawn from the headship of the Holy Roman Empire and from the Catholic Church are misleading. As commander of the believers, the military office of the caliph was emphasized. As *iman*, leader in public prayer, the caliph could and did lead the religious service and pronounce the Friday sermon; but this was a function which the humblest of Moslems could perform. Succession to Muhammad (*khilafah*) meant succession to the sovereignty of the state. Muhammad as a prophet, as an instrument of revelation, as a messenger of Allah, could have no successor. The caliph's relation to religion was merely that of a protector and guardian. He defended the faith just as any European emperor was supposed to, suppressed heresies, warred against unbelievers and extended the boundaries of "the abode of Islam"—in the performance of all of which he employed the power of his secular arm. Not until the latter part of the eighteenth century did the notion prevail in Europe that the Moslem caliph was a kind of pope with spiritual jurisdiction over the followers of Muhammad throughout the world. The shrewd Abd-al-Hamid II made capital of the idea to strengthen his prestige in the eyes of the European powers who had by this time come to dominate most of the Moslems in Asia and Africa. An ill-defined movement had its inception in the latter part of the last century and under the name pan-Islamism exerted special effort to bring about some unity of action to oppose the Christian powers. With Turkey as its rallying point it unduly stressed the ecumenical character of the caliphate.

The one to wrest the caliphate from Ali was a distant cousin, the shrewd Muawiyah, governor of Syria. With him the principle of sovereignty took a new turn: the caliphate became a dynasty, established on the principle of succession, rather than on the principle of casual election as heretofore. There were to be three great dynasties in the period which our story covers: the Umayyad, which now begins in the year 661 with the caliphate of Muawiyah in Damascus; the Abbasid, in Baghdad, which endured from 750 to 1258; and the Fatimid, which ruled from 909 to 1171, with its seat in Cairo. And there was an illustrious branch of the Umayyad caliphate in Spain, from 929 to 1031 with Cordova for its capital. Of these caliphates only the Fatimid claimed descent from Ali. The dynastic principle was to introduce a semblance of political stability. Actually, however, there was seldom a long period when bloody internal warfare did not plague Islam; and there were times when a caliph, though nominally the head of an empire, did not in fact exercise control in his capital city.

Another new note which was to echo more and more loudly in Islam throughout the following centuries was also sounded in the events which accompanied Muawiyah's rise to power. Iraq had declared Ali's son, al-Hasan, the legitimate successor to the throne—with logic, since he was the eldest son of the deceased caliph and Fatimah, the only surviving daughter of the Prophet. But, unfortunately, this grandson of the Prophet had already sojourned too long among the fleshpots. His talents lay in fields other than administration—namely, in the boudoir. Though he died at the age of forty-five, he had by that time succeeded in making and unmaking no less than one hundred marriages and in winning a highly individual title for himself:

"the great divorcer." Consistent, at any rate, in recognizing the true nature of his ability, he genially permitted Muawiyah to buy him off as an aspirant to the caliphate, with a lifetime subsidy.

Muawiyah was a man of unusual administrative skill. And out of chaos he developed an orderly Moslem society. His army was the first disciplined force known in Islamic warfare. Historians credit him also with being the first in Islam to institute a bureau of registry and the first to interest himself in a postal service, which was shortly to develop into a well-organized system knitting together the various parts of the empire.

In Muawiyah the political sense was developed to a degree probably higher than in any other caliph. To his Arab biographers his supreme virtue was his *hilm*, which might be translated as finesse, that unusual ability to resort to force only when force was absolutely necessary and to use peaceful measures in all other instances. His prudent mildness by which he tried to disarm the enemy and shame the opposition, his slowness to anger and his absolute self-control left him under all circumstances master of the situation. "I apply not my sword," he is reported to have declared, "where my lash suffices, nor my lash where my tongue is enough. And even if there be one hair binding me to my fellowmen, I do not let it break: when they pull I loosen, and if they loosen I pull." The following is a letter he is supposed to have forwarded to al-Hasan on the occasion of the latter's abdication: "I admit that because of thy blood relationship thou art more entitled to this high office than I. And if I were sure of thy greater ability to fulfill the duties involved I would unhesitatingly swear allegiance to thee. Now then, ask what thou wilt." Enclosed was a blank for al-Hasan to fill in, already signed by Muawiyah. The would-be rival was naturally enchanted by such an offer.

As succeeding caliphs were to do, Muawiyah measured swords with the Byzantines and twice stretched out his strong arm against Constantinople itself. During his governorship of Syria, a Moslem fleet challenged Byzantine sea power in a sanguinary engagement off the Lycian coast in Asia Minor, registering the first great naval victory of Islam. Constantinople, then and later—until the time of the Turks—proved to be impregnable. Nor did the Arabs ever manage to obtain a permanent foothold in Asia Minor, or to span the Hellespont. It was eastward and westward, along the lines of least resistance, that their main energy was directed. In the time of Muawiyah they were again on the march.

Conquest of Spain

The acquisition of Syria, Iraq, Persia and Egypt brought to an end the first stage in the history of Moslem conquest. A short period of civil disturbances followed. The second stage now begins.

A whirlwind campaign in the east carried the banner of the Prophet across the Oxus River, the traditional boundary line between Persian-speaking and Turkish-speaking peoples, and on to outer Mongolia. Bukhara, Tashkand, Samarqand, storied cities of medieval times, capitulated to the Moslems, and the supremacy of Islam in Central Asia was so firmly established that the Chinese ceased to dispute it. Another eastern column moved south, through the territory which is now termed Baluchistan, and in the year 712 reduced Sind, the lower valley and delta of the Indus River. The conquest was extended as far as Multan in southern Panjab, the seat of a renowned shrine of the Buddha, and the Indian border provinces were forever Islamized. These conquests materialized a few years ago in the state of Pakistan. Here Islam established contact with a new culture, that of Buddhism.

On the north-central front the Arab wave broke, as always, against the citadel of Constantinople, this period witnessing the memorable year-long siege of the Byzantine capital—August 716 to September 717—in which the passage of the Arab fleet into the Golden Horn was barred by a great chain.

But it was westward that the Moslems swept forward to their most spectacular triumph. They had already penetrated North Africa to the site of ancient Carthage. Under one of Islam's most puissant generals, Musa ibn-Nusayr, they passed on through the land of the Berbers, a racial group belonging to the Hamitic branch of the white race, probably in prehistoric times of the same stock as the Semites. Most of the Berbers on the coast had become Christians. Tertullian, St. Cyprian and above all St. Augustine, princes among the early Christian fathers, stemmed from here. But inward from the coast the native population had not been deeply touched by Roman or Byzantine civilization, a culture quite alien to the mentality of these nomadic and seminomadic North Africans.

Islam had a special attraction for people in a cultural stage such as that of the Berbers, and the Semitic Arabs readily established intimate relations with their Hamitic cousins. Islam once again performed its seeming miracle of Arabicizing and Islamizing the religion of a semi-barbarous horde. The blood of the conquerors found fresh ethnic strains for its enrichment, the Arabic tongue a vast field for conquest and rising Islam a new foothold in its climb toward world supremacy.

In its swiftness of execution and completeness of success the expedition into Spain holds a unique place in medieval military annals. The first reconnaissance was made in July 710, when four hundred foot and one hundred horse —all Berbers and soldiers of Musa, the governor of North Africa under the Umayyads—landed on the tiny peninsula (Tarifa) which is almost the southernmost tip of the European continent.

Musa, who had held the governorship since about 699, had driven the Byzantines forever from the territory west of Carthage and had gradually pushed his conquests to the Atlantic, thus acquiring for Islam a *point d'appui* for the invasion of Europe. Encouraged by the success of the first raid and by the dynastic trouble in the Visigothic kingdom of Spain and actuated more by the desire for booty than for conquest, Musa in 711 dispatched his Berber freedman Tariq into Spain with 7,000 men, most of whom were Berbers. Tariq landed near the mighty rock which has since immortalized his name (Jabal [mount of] Tariq), Gibraltar, where the strait is only thirteen miles wide. The ships, so the tra-

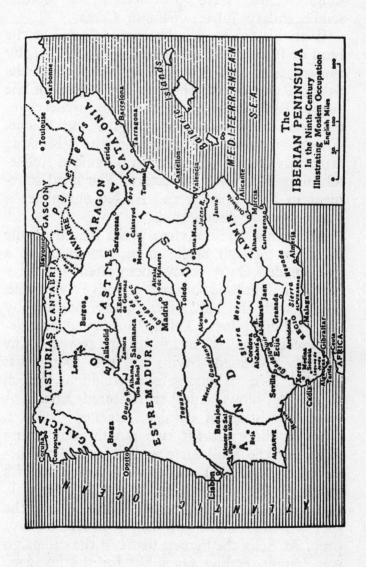

The
IBERIAN PENINSULA
In the Ninth Century
Illustrating Moslem Occupation
English Miles

dition states, were provided by a certain semilegendary Julian, count of Ceuta.

With his forces supplemented, Tariq, at the head of 12,000 men, was met on July 19, 711, by the armies of King Roderick at the mouth of the Salado River on the shore of the lagoon of the Janda. Roderick had deposed his predecessor, the son of Witiza, and usurped the throne. Though numbering 25,000 men, the Visigothic army was utterly routed. What became of Roderick himself remains a mystery. The usual statement in both Spanish and Arabic chronicles is that he simply disappeared.

After this decisive victory the march of the Moslems through Spain almost amounted to a promenade. Only towns dominated by Visigothic knighthood offered effective resistance. Tariq, with the bulk of the army, heading by way of Ecija toward Toledo, the capital, sent detachments against neighboring towns. The strongly fortified Seville in the south was avoided. One column seized Archidona, which struck no blow. Another captured Elvira. A third, consisting of cavalry, attacked Cordova. After holding out for two months this future capital of the Moslems was delivered to the besiegers, we are told, through the treachery of a shepherd who pointed out a breach in the wall. Malaga offered no resistance. Elvira, close to the spot where Granada now stands, proved an easy prey. At Ecija the fiercest battle of the campaign was fought, ending favorably for the invaders. Toledo, the Visigoths' capital, was betrayed by certain Jewish residents. Thus did Tariq, who in the spring of 711 had started as leader of a raid, become by the end of the summer the master of half of Spain. He had destroyed a whole kingdom.

Jealous of the unexpected and phenomenal success of his lieutenant, Musa himself with 10,000 troops—all Arabians and Syrian Arabs—rushed to Spain in June 712. For his objective he chose those towns and strongholds avoided by Tariq—Medina Sidonia and Carmona. Seville, the largest city and the intellectual center of Spain and once its Roman capital, held out under siege until the end of June 713. But the most obstinate resistance was met at Merida. After a year's beleaguering, however, this city was taken by storm on June 1, 713.

It was in or near Toledo that Musa met Tariq. Here, we are told, he whipped his subordinate and put him in chains for refusing to obey orders to halt in the early stage of the campaign. But the conquest went on. Soon Saragossa, in the north, was reached and the Moslem troops advanced into the highlands of Aragon, Leon, the Asturias and Galicia. In the autumn of the same year the Caliph al-Walid in distant Damascus recalled Musa, charging him with the same offense for which Musa had disciplined his Berber subordinate—acting independently of his superior. As governor of Africa, Musa had none but the caliph for his superior.

Leaving his second son, Abd-al-Aziz, in command of the newly acquired territory, Musa

slowly made his way overland toward Syria. On
his march he was accompanied by his officers,
some four hundred Visigothic princes, wearing
crowns and girdled with gold belts, and followed
by an endless retinue of slaves and prisoners of
war loaded with enormous treasures of booty.
The story of the triumphal passage of this
princely train through northern Africa from
west to east is a favorite with Arab historians. Its
description brings to mind the picture of the ancient victorious marches of Roman generals. The
news of the impressive procession traveled to
Damascus faster than the procession itself. On
reaching Tiberias, Musa found orders awaiting
him from Sulayman, brother and heir of the sick
al-Walid, to delay his advent to the capital. The
caliph-to-be hoped thereby to have the arrival
grace his accession to the throne.

In February 715 Musa entered Damascus with
his Visigothic princes bedecked in their jewelry
and was evidently received with favor by al-
Walid. The official reception, held with great
dignity and pomp in the courtyard of the magnificent Umayyad Mosque, is a gleaming pinna-
cle in the history of triumphant Islam. For the
first time hundreds of Western royalty and thousands of European captives were seen offering
homage to the commander of the believers.

Musa presented the caliph, among other tro-
phies, with the superb table whose workmanship
legend assigns to genii in the service of King Solomon. From Jerusalem this unique piece of art,
legend asserts, was carried away by the Romans

into their capital, whence it was later taken by
the Goths. Each Gothic king vied with the preceding one in decorating the table with precious
stones. The treasure was kept in the cathedral
and was captured by Tariq, probably from the
bishop as he fled with it. When Musa met Tariq
in Toledo and administered his whipping he
also seized the table, but Tariq, so the story goes,
had secreted one of its legs and now in the presence of the caliph dramatically produced the
missing part as proof of his own exploit.

The same fate which befell many another successful Arab general awaited Musa. Al-Walid's
successor humiliated him. Besides disciplining
him by making him stand until exhausted in the
sun, he confiscated his property and deprived
him of all authority. The last we hear of the aged
conqueror of Africa and Spain is as a beggar in
a remote village of Hijaz.

Spain was now a province of the caliphate.
The Arabic name it assumed was al-Andalus.
Etymologically this word is connected with the
name of the Vandals, who had occupied the land
before the Arabs. Musa's immediate successors
had only small territories in the north and east of
the peninsula to conquer and comparatively few
revolts to quell. Within the short space of seven
years the conquest of the peninsula, one of the
fairest and largest provinces of medieval Europe,
was effected. The conquerors were there to stay
—for centuries at least.

The reasons for this seemingly unprecedented
triumph are not hard to discern even from the

above sketchy account. In the first place, the line of national cleavage between the Visigoths (West Goths) who entered Spain in the early part of the fifth century as Teutonic barbarians and the Spanish-Roman population was not yet entirely obliterated. The Goths had to struggle for a long time to displace their predecessors, the Suevi and Vandals, who were likewise invading Germanic hordes. The Visigoths ruled as absolute, often despotic, monarchs. They clung to the Arian form of Christianity until one of them, Recared, in 587 accepted Catholicism, the religion of the natives. As Catholics the people had hated the rule of the heretical Goths. The natives included a considerable class of serfs and slaves, who were naturally dissatisfied with their hard lot. That this enslaved class should have contributed its share to the success of the invasion and cooperated with the invaders is not surprising. Then there was the Jewish element in the population which was estranged from the bulk of the nation through active persecution by the Gothic royalty. Attempts at their forced conversion were consummated by a royal decree issued in 612 enjoining all Jews to be baptized under penalty of banishment and confiscation of property. That explains why several of the conquered towns were left in charge of Jews as the Moslem invaders marched through Spain.

We should, moreover, remember that political disagreements among the royalty and nobility of the Goths themselves, coupled with internal strife, had undermined the state. Toward the end of the sixth century the Gothic nobles had become territorial lords. The Moslem invasion coincided with the accession to the throne of a usurper from among the nobility who was readily betrayed by the kinsmen of his deposed predecessor. On the conquest of Toledo, Achila, the deposed son of Witiza, who had naïvely cherished the notion that the Arabs were fighting his battle for him, contented himself with the recovery of his estates in Toledo. Here he continued to live in great pomp. His uncle, Bishop Oppas, was installed over the metropolitan see of the capital. As for Julian, the governor of Ceuta who is supposed to have provided the Arab army with boats, the part he played in the conquest was greatly exaggerated.

The fall of Saragossa removed one of the last barriers between Spain and France. But there remained the Pyrenees. Musa never crossed them, though certain Arab chroniclers credit him with the feat and with having even entertained the hope of traversing "the land of the Franks" and joining hands through Constantinople with the caliph in Damascus. Though wild and fantastic, the dream of fighting their way through Europe may have flashed through the brains of the Arab invaders, whose knowledge of the geography of Europe could not have been great. In reality it was Musa's third successor, al-Hurr ibn-Abd-al-Rahman al-Thaqafi, who, in 717 or 718, was the first to cross the range.

Lured by the rich treasures of the convents and churches of France and encouraged by the

89

internal dissension between the chief officers of
the Merovingian court and the dukes of Aquitaine, al-Hurr started the raids which were continued by his successor al-Samh ibn-Malik al-
Khawlani. In 720, al-Samh seized Septimania,
which was a dependency of the defunct Visigothic kingdom, and captured Narbonne, which
was converted later into a huge citadel with an
arsenal and depots for provisions and arms. But
his attempt in the following year at Toulouse,
the seat of Duke Eudes of Aquitaine, resulted in
failure, thanks to the effective resistance offered.
Here al-Samh "suffered martyrdom," i.e. fell in
battle against non-Moslems. The first great victory by a Germanic prince over Moslems had
been won. The subsequent movements of the
Arabs beyond the Pyrenees were not successful.

The last and greatest expedition northward
was led by Abd-al-Rahman ibn-Abdullah al-
Ghafiqi, successor of al-Samh as governor over
Spain. Abd-al-Rahman advanced through the
western Pyrenees, which he crossed in the early
spring of 732. Having vanquished Duke Eudes
on the banks of the Garonne, he stormed Bor-
deaux, setting its churches on fire. After burning
a basilica outside the walls of Poitiers he pushed
northward to the vicinity of Tours. As the rest-
ing place of the body of St. Martin, the apostle
of the Gauls, Tours was a sort of religious capital
for Gaul. Its votive offerings undoubtedly presented the chief attraction to the invaders.

Here, between Tours and Poitiers, at the junc-
tion of the Clain and the Vienne, Abd-al-Rah-

man was met by Charles Martel, mayor of the palace at the Merovingian court, whose aid Eudes had besought. Charles, as the surname Martel (the hammer) which he later won signifies, was valiant and bold. He had subdued many enemies and obliged Eudes, who exercised independent authority in Aquitaine, to acknowledge the nominal sovereignty of the northern Franks. Though not king in name Charles, an illegitimate son of Pepin of Heristal, was king in fact.

For seven days the Arab army under Abd-al-Rahman and the Frankish forces under Charles, mostly foot soldiers clad in wolfskins with long matted hair hanging down over their shoulders, stood facing one another anxiously awaiting the moment of joining battle. Light skirmishes dragged on. At last, on an October Saturday of 732, the Arab leader took the initiative in the attack. The Frankish warriors, who in the heat of the fight had formed a hollow square, stood shoulder to shoulder, firm as a wall, inflexible as a block of ice—in the words of a Western historian. The light cavalry of the enemy failed against them. Without giving way they hewed down with their swords all attackers. Among the victims was Abd-al-Rahman himself. Darkness at last separated the combatants. At the dawn of the day the stillness of the hostile camp caused Charles to suspect a ruse. Spies were sent out to ascertain the facts. Under cover of night the Arabs had quietly deserted their tents and vanished. Charles was victorious.

Later legends embellished this day of Poitiers

or Tours, greatly exaggerating its historic importance. To the Christians it meant the turning point in the military fortunes of their eternal foe. Gibbon, and after him other historians, would see mosques in Paris and London, where cathedrals now stand, and would hear the Koran instead of the Bible expounded in Oxford and other seats of learning, had the Arabs won the day. To several modern historical writers this battle of Tours is one of the decisive battles in history.

In reality the battle of Tours decided nothing. The Arab-Berber wave, already almost a thousand miles from its starting place in Gibraltar, had reached a natural standstill. It had lost its momentum and spent itself. Internal discord and jealousy between its two component racial elements were beginning to tell on the morale of Abd-al-Rahman's army. Among the Arabs themselves there was no unanimity of feeling and purpose. It is true that the Moslems were checked at this point, but their raids continued elsewhere. In 734, for instance, they seized Avignon; nine years later they pillaged Lyons; and not until 759 did they relinquish their hold on Narbonne, the strategic base of their operations. Although this defeat near Tours was not the actual cause of the Arab halt, it does set the farthest limit of the victorious Moslem arms.

The year 732 marked the first centennial of the Prophet's death. His followers were now the conquerors of an empire extending from the Bay of Biscay to the Indus and the frontiers of China, from the Aral Sea to the upper Nile. Damascus, which young Muhammad according to tradition hesitated to enter because he wished to see Paradise only once, had become the capital of this huge empire. In the heart of the city stood the glittering palace of the Umayyads, commanding a view of flourishing plains which extended southwestward to Mount Hermon with its turban of perpetual snow. Its builder was none other than Muawiyah, founder of the dynasty, and it stood beside the Umayyad Mosque which al-Walid had newly adorned and made into that jewel of architecture which still attracts lovers of beauty. In the audience chamber a square seat covered with richly embroidered cushions formed the caliphal throne, on which during formal audiences the caliph, in flowing robes, sat cross-legged. On the right stood his paternal relatives in a row according to seniority, on the left his maternal relatives. Courtiers, poets and petitioners stood behind. The more formal audiences were held in the glorious Umayyad Mosque, even at the present day one of the most magnificent places of worship in the world. In some such setting must the Caliph al-Walid have received Musa and Tariq, the conquerors of Spain, with their prisoners and treasures. The march of Islam had reached its climax and the glory of Islam's first dynasty had reached its zenith.

Social and Cultural Life
Makes a Start

We have come to the end of the first major phase of our story. The march of Islam has ended. Although there was unending warfare within the empire to the day the empire was no more, the burden of our narrative shifts now from the story of battles and conquest to the far more significant and in many ways more exciting story of the march of ideas, of the development of culture within the Moslem empire, the rise of literature, science, medicine, art and architecture and the heartening chronicle of how, through the interpenetration of cultures, man passes on to the triumphs of his mind when the victories of the sword have fallen away.

It is a striking fact that in its general tone and character, life in the Damascus of the eighth century was not greatly different from what it is today. Then, as now, in the narrow, covered streets the Damascene with his wide trousers, red pointed shoes and huge turban could be seen rubbing shoulders with the suntanned Bedouin in his loose gown surmounted by head shawl and head band, and occasionally meeting a European-dressed *Ifranji*, or Frank, as all Europeans are still called. Here and there the aristocrat, the well-to-do Damascene, might be seen on horseback cloaked in a white silk 'aba and armed with a sword or lance. A few women, all veiled, cross the streets; others stealthily peep through the latticed windows of their homes overlooking the bazars and public squares. Sherbet sellers and sweet-meat vendors raise their voices to the highest pitch in competition with the incessant tramp of the passers-by and the multitude of donkeys and camels laden with the varied products of the desert and the sown land. The city atmosphere is charged with smells—every conceivable odor under the sun.

As in other cities the Arabians lived in separate quarters of their own according to their tribal affiliation. In Damascus (Dimashq), Hims, Aleppo and other towns these quarters are still well marked. The doorway of each house opened from the street into a courtyard in the center of which usually stood a large water basin with a flowing jet emitting from time to time a veil-like spray. An orange or citron tree grew by the basin. The rooms surrounded the courtyard, which in larger houses was provided with a cloister. It is to the eternal glory of the Umayyads

95

that they supplied Damascus with a water system which was unexcelled in the contemporary Orient and still continues to function.

The population throughout the empire was divided into four social classes. The highest consisted naturally of the ruling Moslems headed by the caliphal household and the aristocracy of Arabian conquerors. Exactly how numerous was this class cannot be ascertained; it embraced in Hims and Damascus from 20,000 to 45,000 people.

Next below the Arabian Moslems came the Neo-Moslems, who by force or persuasion had professed Islam and were thereby admitted in theory, though not in practice, to the full rights of Islamic citizenship. A Moslem was supposed to pay no tribute. Here Arabian chauvinism, pitted against theoretical claims, proved too strong for those claims to be realized. There is no doubt that throughout practically all the period of the Umayyads, holders of land, whether believers or unbelievers, were made to pay land tax. Yet one of the causes for the decline of state revenue was undoubtedly conversion to Islam.

Reduced to the position of "clients," these neophyte Moslems formed the lowest stratum of Moslem society, a status which they bitterly resented. This explains our finding them in many cases espousing such causes as the Shiite in Iraq or the Kharijite in Persia, sects which were to cause unending dissension and bloodshed. Some of them, however, as often happens, proved religiously "more royal than the king," and their zeal for the new faith, bordering on fanaticism, made them persecute non-Moslems. Among the most intolerant early Moslems are numbered converts from Christianity and Judaism.

Within the Moslem society these clients were naturally the first to devote themselves to learned studies and fine arts, for they represented the longer tradition of culture. As they outshone the Moslem Arabians in the intellectual field they began to contest with them for political leadership. Through their intermarriages with the conquering stock they served to dilute the Arabian blood and ultimately to make that element inconspicuous amidst the mixture of varied racial strains.

The third class was made up of members of tolerated sects, professors of revealed religions, the so-called "*dhimmis*," the Christians, Jews and Sabians with whom the Moslems had made covenant. This recognition of tolerated religions, whose devotees were to be disarmed and compelled to pay tribute in return for Moslem protection, was one of the chief political innovations of Muhammad and was largely due to the esteem in which the Prophet held the Bible and partly to the aristocratic connections of certain Christian tribes.

In this status the dhimmis enjoyed considerable freedom from the payment of land and capitation taxes. Even in matters of civil and criminal judicial procedure, except where a Moslem was involved, these people were practically under their own spiritual heads. Moslem law was too sacred to be applicable to them. Essential parts of this system were still in force as late as the Ottoman period and have survived to the mandatory days of Syria and Palestine.

At the bottom of society stood the slaves. Islam preserved the ancient Semitic institution of slavery, the legality of which the Old Testament admitted, but it appreciably ameliorated the condition of the slave. Canon law forbade the Moslem to enslave his coreligionist, but promised no liberty to an alien slave who adopted Islam. Slaves in early Islam were recruited from prisoners of war, including women and children, unless ransomed, and by purchase or raiding. Soon the slave trade became very brisk and lucrative in all Moslem lands. Some slaves from East or Central Africa were black; others from Chinese Turkestan were yellow; still others from the Near East or from eastern and southern Europe were white. The Spanish slaves brought about a thousand dinars each, while Turkish slaves were worth only six hundred. According to Islamic law the offspring of a female slave by another slave, by any man other than her master, or by her master in case he did not acknowledge the fatherhood of the child, was likewise a slave; but the offspring of a male slave by a freewoman was free.

An idea of the number of slaves flooding the Moslem empire as a result of conquest may be gained from such exaggerated figures as the following: Musa took 300,000 captives from North Africa, one-fifth of whom he forwarded to the caliph, and from the Gothic nobility in Spain he captured 30,000 virgins; the captives of one Moslem general in Turkestan alone numbered 100,000.

Between the master and the female slave, concubinage was permissible, but not legal marriage. The children of such a union belonged to the master and were therefore free; but the status of the concubine was thereby raised only to that of "mother of children," who could neither be sold by her husband-master nor given away, and who at his death was declared free. In the melting-pot process which resulted in the amalgamation of Arabians and foreigners, the slave trade undoubtedly played an extremely important role.

We have noted that the invaders from the desert brought with them no tradition of learning, no heritage of culture, to the lands they conquered. The closeness of the Umayyad period to the "barbarian" age, its many wars, and the unsettled social and economic conditions of the Moslem world all militated against the possibility of intellectual development in that early epoch. But the seed was then sown and the tree of knowledge which came into full bloom under the next dynasty in Baghdad certainly had its roots in this preceding period of Greek, Syrian and Persian culture. The Umayyad age was in general one of incubation.

As Persians, Syrians, Copts, Berbers and others flocked to the fold of Islam and married Arabians, the original high wall raised earlier between Arabians and non-Arabians tumbled down. The nationality of the Moslem receded into the background. No matter what his nationality may have been originally, the follower of Muhammad now passed for an Arab. An Arab henceforth became one who professed Islam and spoke and wrote the Arabic tongue, regardless of his racial affiliation. This is one of the most significant facts in the history of Islamic civilization. The Arabic-speaking man, hitherto but an Arabian, has thus become international. When we therefore speak of "Arab medicine" or "Arab philosophy" or "Arab mathematics" we do not mean the medical science, philosophy or mathematics that are necessarily the product of the Arabian mind or developed by people living in the Arabian peninsula, but that body of knowledge enshrined in books written in the Arabic language by men who flourished chiefly during the caliphate and were themselves Persians, Syrians, Egyptians or Arabians, Christian, Jewish or Moslem, and who may have drawn some of their material from Greek, Aramaean, Indo-Persian or other sources.

On the borderland of Persia the scientific study of the Arabic language and grammar was begun and carried on mainly for foreign converts and partly by them. The first impulse came from the desire to supply the linguistic needs of Neo-Moslems who wanted to study the Koran, hold government positions and converse with the conquerors. The original grammatical treatise was, according to legend, drawn up on a caliph's dictum that "the parts of speech are three: noun, verb and particle." Arabic grammar, however, shows long and slow development and bears striking marks of the influence of Greek logic.

The study of the Koran and the necessity of expounding it gave rise to the twin sciences of philology and lexicography, as well as to that most characteristically Moslem literary activity —the science of tradition—*hadith*, literally "narrative." In its technical sense a tradition is an act or saying attributed to the Prophet or to one of his companions. The Koran and tradition provided the foundation upon which theology and law were raised. Law in Islam is more intimately related to religion than to jurisprudence as modern lawyers understand it. Roman law, directly or through the Talmud and other media, did undoubtedly affect Umayyad legislation, but to what extent has not been fully ascertained.

This period saw the beginning of Arab science, the first treatise on medicine coming, characteristically, by way of a translation by a Jew of a Greek tract composed by a Christian priest in Alexandria. Alchemy, like medicine, one of the few sciences in which the Arabs later made a distinct contribution, was one of the disciplines early developed.

Poetry and music flourished in the court at Damascus, the latter over the protest of conservatives, who linked music and song with wine-drinking and gambling as diversions forbidden by the Prophet. The greatest measure of intellectual progress achieved under the Umayyads was undoubtedly in the field of poetical composition.

101

The preceding grim period of conquest had inspired no poet in a nation of poets, but with the accession of the worldly Umayyads the old connections with the goddesses of wine, song and poetry were reestablished. For the first time the poet of love makes his full appearance in Arabic.

In the case of the Moslem Arabs, art found its supreme expression in religious architecture. The Moslem architects, or the men they employed, evolved a scheme of building, simple and dignified, based on earlier patterns but singularly expressive of the spirit of the new religion. Thus we have in the mosque (from *masjid*, meaning a placc to prostrate oneself) an epitome of the history of the development of Islamic civilization in its interracial and international relationships. Perhaps no clearer example could be cited to illustrate the cultural interplay between Islam and its neighbors than the mosque.

The simple mosque of Muhammad at Medina became the general prototype of the congregational mosque in the first century of Islam. This mosque consisted of a courtyard open to the sky, enclosed by walls of sun-baked clay. As a protection from the sun the Prophet later extended the flat roof from the adjacent buildings over the whole open court. The roof consisted of palm trunks used as columns to support a cover of palm fronds and mud. A palm trunk fixed in the ground served first as a pulpit for the Prophet to stand on while addressing the congregation. This was later replaced by a small platform of tamarisk wood with three steps copied from those seen in

Christian churches in Syria. Here, then, we have in their simplest forms almost all the rudiments of a congregational mosque—a court, some cover to shelter the worshiper and a pulpit.

The subsequent advance of the Arabians fanwise through Western Asia and North Africa brought them into possession of numberless standing and ruined structures representing a high artistic development and, what is more essential, it put them in control of the living technical knowledge and skill inherited by members of the conquered races from ages past. This technique, applied to the religious needs of the Moslem community, produced in course of time what has been variously designated Saracenic, Arabian, Moslem and Muhammadan art. Moslems object to the use of the term "Muhammadan" because of its parallelism to the term "Christian" applied to the worshipers of Christ, for they, as they maintain, are not worshipers of Muhammad.

Because of its biblical association and as the traditional stopping place of Muhammad on his celebrated nocturnal journey heavenward, Jerusalem very early acquired special sanctity in the eyes of all Moslems. The Dome of the Rock, built in 691 on a spot hallowed by Jewish, heathen, Christian and Moslem associations and considered by tradition the place where Abraham intended to sacrifice his son Isaac, shows a radical change from the old pattern, involving the introduction of mosaic and other decorative motifs and a dome erected to surpass the beautiful cupola of the Church of the Holy Sepulchre. The result was an architectural monument of such noble beauty that it has scarcely been surpassed anywhere.

The great mosque in Damascus shows even more plainly how "Arab civilization" developed. In 705 the Caliph al-Walid had taken over the site of the Christian basilica of Damascus dedicated to St. John, originally a temple of Jupiter, and built there the grand mosque named after the Umayyads. How much of the Christian construction was preserved in al-Walid's mosque is difficult to ascertain. The two southern minarets stand on ancient church towers which belonged to the old basilica, but the northern minaret, used as a beacon tower, was certainly constructed by al-Walid and became the model for similar structures in Syria, North Africa and Spain. It is the oldest purely Moslem minaret surviving. This caliph employed Persian and Indian craftsmen as well as Greek artisans provided by the emperor of Constantinople. Papyri recently discovered show that material and skilled workmen were imported from Egypt.

From the above and what follows it is apparent that the Arab, having given the world a lesson in the art of war, was also ready to learn the arts of peace and capable of achieving victory in them.

The Glory That Was Baghdad

The Arabs addressed themselves to the task of mastering the depravities of the civilized life of the time with no less ardor than they studied its esthetics and learning. Shortly before the middle of the eighth century a caliph ascended to the Umayyad throne who had been born of a slave mother—a portentous fact. His two successors, the last in the dynasty, were also sons of slave women. The eunuch system, which made the harem institution possible, was now fully developed. Indulgence in luxury was rife due to increased wealth and a superabundance of slaves. That the reigning family could no longer boast pure Arab blood was symptomatic of a loosening of moral standards throughout society.

The position of the Umayyad dynasty, weakened by this decadence, was further undermined by the increasingly sharp division of North Arabian as against South Arabian tribes. This racial tendency to separatism, apparent even in pre-Islamic days, now became complete and was the cause of boundless dispute. Everywhere, on the banks of the Indus, the shores of Sicily and the borders of the Sahara, the ancestral feud, transformed into an alignment of two political parties, called Qays and Yaman, made itself felt. In Lebanon and Palestine the issue remained a living one until modern times, for we know of pitched battles fought between the two parties as late as the eighteenth century.

The lack of any definite and fixed rule of heredity succession to the caliphal throne weakened the dynasty still further. Muawiyah had initiated the wise and farsighted policy of nominating his son as his successor, but the antiquated Arabian principle of seniority in succession stood in constant conflict with the natural ambition of the ruling father to pass the sovereignty on to his son.

Significantly, and paradoxically—since in the chronicles of the day "the people" are scarcely even mentioned—homage by the people became the only sure title to the throne. This homage was expressed through the leaders. But the day when the people of any state, as the ultimate repository of sovereign power, could make their wishes known other than by haphazard mob action lay far in the future.

In 747 open revolt against the Umayyads was proclaimed by their cousins the Abbasids, de-

scendants of an uncle of the Prophet, al-Abbas.
It was successful. The Umayyad house was ex-
terminated. One Abbasid general invited eighty
leading members of the deposed house to a banquet, in the course of the feast had them all cut
down, and after spreading leathern covers over
the dead and dying, continued his repast. The
first Abbasid caliph referred to himself as *al-
saffah*, "the bloodshedder," which became his
sobriquet. The fact was ominous. The incoming
dynasty depended upon force in the execution of
its policies. For the first time in the history of
Islam the leathern spread beside the caliph's seat,
which served as a carpet for the executioner,
became a necessary adjunct of the imperial
throne. The Abbasid caliphs never controlled
North Africa or Spain but they did rule over the
eastern part of the Islamic world for the next five
hundred years, until the thirty-seventh caliph of
the line met his destruction at the hands of the
Mongols in 1258. It was under the Abbasids that
Islamic civilization experienced its golden age.

Baghdad was the creation of the Abbasids, the
city which the second ruler of the dynasty had
caused to be built on the west bank of the Tigris
River, in that same valley which had furnished
sites for some of the mightiest capitals of the ancient world. "It is an excellent military camp,"
he had remarked. "Besides, here is the Tigris to
put us in touch with lands as far as China and
bring us all that the seas yield as well as the food
products of Mesopotamia, Armenia and their environs. Then there is the Euphrates to carry for

us all that Syria, al-Raqqah and adjacent lands have to offer." It was a sagacious choice, and the new city—on the construction of which one hundred thousand laborers, craftsmen and architects worked for four years—instantly flourished.

The city was circular in form—whence the name the Round City—with double brick walls, a deep moat and a third innermost wall rising ninety feet and surrounding the central area. The walls had four gates from which four highways, starting from the center of the circle, radiated like the spokes of a wheel to the four corners of the empire. The whole thus formed concentric circles with the caliphal palace—styled the Golden Gate or the Green Dome—as the hub. Beside the palace stood the great mosque. The dome of the audience chamber, from which the imperial palace was named, rose to a height of one hundred and thirty feet. Later tradition topped it by the figure of a mounted man holding a lance that in time of danger pointed the direction from which the enemy might be expected. But an Arab geographer remarks that the figure necessarily pointed always in the same direction, which would mean the existence of a constant enemy threatening the city, and declares the Moslems "too intelligent to believe such fabrications."

The new location opened the way for ideas from the East. Arab Islam succumbed to Persian influence; the caliphate became more a revival of Iranian despotism and less an Arabian sheikhdom. Gradually Persian titles, Persian wines and wives, Persian mistresses, Persian songs, as well as Persian ideas and thoughts, won the day. Their influence softened the rough edges of the primitive Arabian life and paved the way for a new era distinguished by the cultivation of science and scholarly pursuits. In two fields only did the Arabian hold his own: Islam remained the religion of the state and Arabic continued to be the official language of the state registers.

The ninth century opened with two imperial names standing supreme in world affairs: Charlemagne in the West and the Caliph Harun al-Rashid in the East. Of the two, Harun was undoubtedly the more powerful and represented the higher culture. The two contemporaries entered into friendly relations, prompted, of course, by self-interest. Charlemagne cultivated Harun as a possible ally against hostile Byzantium. Harun desired to use Charlemagne against his rivals and deadly foes, the neighboring Umayyads of Spain, who had succeeded in establishing a mighty and prosperous state. This reciprocity of cordial feelings found expression, according to Western writers, in the exchange of a number of embassies and presents. A Frankish author who is sometimes referred to as Charlemagne's secretary relates that the envoys of the great king of the West returned home with rich gifts from "the king of Persia, Aaron," which included fabrics, aromatics and an elephant. This account speaks further of an intricate clock as among the gifts from Baghdad. The account of the pipe organ sent to Charlemagne by Harun, like many other charming bits of history, is fictitious. Its story is apparently based on a mistranslation of the term *clepsydra* in the sources, which in reality meant a device for measuring time by water and referred to the clock presented. Likewise the story that the keys of the Church of the Holy Sepulchre were sent by the caliph himself to Charlemagne has been discredited. The strange thing about this exchange of embassies and gifts, said to have taken place between 797 and 806, is the utter silence of Moslem authors regarding it. While reference is made to various other diplomatic exchanges and courtesies, none is made to this.

Though less than half a century old, Baghdad by the time of Harun, 786-809, had grown from nothingness to a world center of prodigious wealth and international significance, standing alone as the rival of Byzantium. Its splendor had kept pace with the prosperity of the empire of which it was the capital. It had become "a city with no peer throughout the whole world."

The royal palace with its many annexes for harems, eunuchs and special functionaries occupied one-third of the Round City. Particularly impressive was its audience chamber with its rugs, curtains and cushions, the best the Orient could produce. The caliph's cousin-wife, Zubaydah, who in tradition shares with her husband the halo of glory and distinction bestowed by later generations, would tolerate at her table no vessels not made of gold or silver and studded with gems. She was the first to ornament her shoes with precious stones. On one holy pilgrimage she is reported to have spent three million dinars, which included the expense of furnishing the city of Mecca with water from a stream twenty-five miles away.

Zubaydah had a rival in the beauteous Ulayyah, half-sister of Harun, who to cover a blemish on her forehead devised a fillet set with jewels which, as the fillet *à la* Ulayyah, was soon adopted by the world of fashion as the ornament of the day.

Especially on ceremonial occasions, such as the installation of the caliph, weddings, pilgrimages and receptions for foreign envoys, did the courtly wealth and magnificence make its fullest display. The marriage ceremony of the Caliph al-Mamun to the eighteen-year-old Buran, daughter of his vizir, was celebrated in 825 with such fabulous expenditure of money that it has lived in Arabic literature as one of the unforgettable extravaganzas of the age. At the nuptials a thousand pearls of unique size, we are told, were showered from a gold tray upon the couple who stood on a golden mat studded with pearls and sapphires. A two-hundred-rotl candle of ambergris turned the night into day. Balls of musk, each containing a ticket naming an estate or a slave or some such gift, were showered on the royal princes and dignitaries. In 917 the caliph al-Muqtadir received in his palace with great ceremony and pomp the envoys of the young Constantine VII, whose mission evidently involved the exchange and ransom of prisoners. The caliphal array included 160,000 cavalry and footmen, 7,000 black and white eunuchs and 700 chamberlains. In the parade a hundred lions marched, and in the caliphal palace hung 38,000 curtains of which 12,500 were gilded, besides 22,000 rugs. The envoys were so struck with awe and admiration that they first mistook the chamberlain's office and then the vizir's for the royal audience chamber. Especially impressed were they with the Hall of the Tree which housed an artificial tree of gold and silver weighing 500,000 drams, in the branches of which were lodged automaton singing birds of the same precious metals. In the garden they marveled at the artificially dwarfed palm trees which by skilled cultivation yielded dates of rare varieties.

Harun was the beau ideal of Islamic kingship. Like a magnet, his princely munificence and that of his immediate successors attracted to the capital poets, wits, musicians, singers, dancers, trainers of fighting dogs and cocks and others who could interest or entertain. The libertine poet abu-Nuwas, the boon companion of al-Rashid and his comrade on many a nocturnal adventure, has depicted for us in unforgettable terms the colorful court life of this period of glory. The pages of *al-Aghani* abound with illustrative anecdotes whose nucleus of truth is not hard to discern. According to one story the Caliph al-Amin, Harun's son, one evening bestowed on his uncle

Ibrahim, a professional singer, the sum of 300,000 dinars for chanting a few verses of abu-Nuwas. This raised the gratuities thus far received by Ibrahim from the caliph to 20,000,000 dirhams, all of which did not amount to more than the land tax of a few districts. For his parties on the Tigris, al-Amin had built a number of special barges shaped like animals. One of these vessels looked like a dolphin, another like a lion, a third like an eagle. The cost of one was 3,000,000 dirhams. We read in the *Aghani* of a picturesque all-night ballet, conducted under the Caliph al-Amin's personal direction, in which a large number of beautiful girl dancers performed in rhythmic unison to the soft harmony of music and were joined in their singing by all those who attended. Another author relates that on the occasion of a dinner given by Ibrahim in honor of his brother al-Rashid, the caliph was served with a dish of fish in which the slices looked exceedingly small. In explanation the host stated that the slices were fishes' tongues, and the waiter added that the cost of the hundred and fifty tongues in the dish was over a thousand dirhams. Even when stripped of the glow cast by Oriental romance and fancy, enough of the splendor of court life in Baghdad remains to arouse our astonishment.

Along Baghdad's miles of wharves lay hundreds of vessels, including ships of war and pleasure craft and varying from Chinese junks to native rafts of inflated sheepskins, not unlike those of our present day, which were floated down from Mosul. Into the bazars of the city came porcelain, silk and musk from China; spices, minerals and dyes from India and the Malay Archipelago; rubies, lapis lazuli, fabrics and slaves from the lands of the Turks in Central Asia; honey, wax, furs and white slaves from Scandinavia and Russia; ivory, gold dust and black slaves from eastern Africa. Chinese wares had a special bazar devoted to their sale. The provinces of the empire itself sent by caravan or sea their domestic products: rice, grain and linen from Egypt; glass, metalware and fruits from Syria; brocade, pearls and weapons from Arabia; silks, perfumes and vegetables from Persia.

From Baghdad and other export centers, Arab merchants shipped to the Far East, Europe and Africa fabrics, jewelry, metal mirrors, glass beads and spices. The hoards of Arab coins recently found in places as far north as Russia, Finland, Sweden and Germany testify to the worldwide commercial activity of the Moslems of this and the later period. The adventures of Sindbad the Sailor, which form one of the best-known tales in *The Thousand and One Nights*, have long been recognized as based upon actual reports of voyages made by Moslem merchants.

Merchants played a leading part in the Baghdad community. Members of each craft and trade had their shops in the same market as in the present day. The monotony of street life was interrupted from time to time by the occasional passage of a wedding or circumcision procession. Professional men—physicians, lawyers, teachers,

114

writers and the like—began to occupy a conspicuous place. A biographer has left us a picture of
the daily routine of a member of the learned fra-
ternity, which indicates that scholarship had a
considerable market value in those days. We are
first shown this man of learning after his daily
ride, at the public bath, where attendants poured
water over him. On emerging he put on a loung-
ing-robe, sipped a drink, ate a biscuit and lay
down, sometimes falling asleep. The siesta over,
he burned perfume to fumigate his person and
ordered a dinner which generally consisted of
soup, fattened chicken and bread. Then he re-
sumed his sleep and on waking drank four rotls
of old wine, to which he might add quinces and
Syrian apples.

The luxurious scale of living made this period
popular in history and in fiction, but what has
rendered it especially illustrious in world annals
is the fact that it witnessed the most momentous
intellectual awakening in the history of Islam and
one of the most significant in the whole history
of thought and culture. The awakening was due
in large measure to foreign influences, partly
Indo-Persian and Syrian but mainly Hellenic,
and was marked by translations into Arabic from
Persian, Sanskrit, Syriac and Greek. Starting
with very little science, philosophy or literature
of his own, the Arabian Moslem, who brought
with him from the desert a keen sense of intellectual curiosity and many latent faculties, soon became, as we have learned before, the beneficiary

and heir of the older and more cultured peoples whom he conquered or encountered. Just as in Syria he adopted the existing Aramaic civilization, itself influenced by the later Greek, so did he in Iraq adopt the same civilization influenced by the Persian. Three-quarters of a century after the establishment of Baghdad the Arabic-reading world was in possession of the chief philosophical works of Aristotle, of the leading Neo-Platonic commentators, and of most of the medical writings of Galen, as well as of Persian and Indian scientific works. In only a few decades the Arabs assimilated what had taken the Greeks centuries to develop. In absorbing the main features of both Hellenic and Persian cultures, Islam lost most of its own original character, which breathed the spirit of the desert and bore the stamp of Arabian nationalism, but thereby took an important place in the medieval cultural unit which linked southern Europe with the Near East. This culture, it should be remembered, was fed by a single stream, a stream with sources in ancient Egypt, Babylonia, Phoenicia and Judea, all flowing to Greece and now returning to the East in the form of Hellenism. We shall see later how this same stream was rediverted into Europe by the Arabs in Spain and Sicily, where it helped create the Renaissance of Europe.

India acted as an early source of inspiration, especially in wisdom literature and mathematics. About 773 an Indian traveler introduced into Baghdad a treatise on astronomy, which by order of the caliph was translated by al-Fazari into Arabic. The stars had of course interested the Arabians since desert days, but no scientific study of them was undertaken until this time. Islam added its impetus to the study of astronomy as a means for fixing the direction in which prayer should be conducted. The famous al-Khwarizmi, who died about 850, based his widely known astronomical tables on al-Fazari's work and syncretized the Indian and Greek systems of astronomy, at the same time adding his own contribution. This same Indian traveler had also brought a treatise on mathematics by means of which the numerals called in Europe Arabic and by the Arabs Indian entered the Moslem world. Later, in the ninth century, the Indians made another important contribution to Arabic mathematical science, the decimal system.

At the time of the Arab conquest of the Fertile Crescent the intellectual legacy of Greece was unquestionably the most precious treasure at hand. Hellenism consequently became the most vital of all foreign influences in Arab life.

The height of Greek influence was reached under al-Mamun. The rationalistic tendencies of this caliph led him to the philosophical works of the Greeks for justification of his position that religious texts should agree with the judgments of reason. In 830 he established in Baghdad his famous "house of wisdom," a combination library, academy and translation bureau which in many respects proved the most important educational institution since the foundation of the

Alexandrian Museum in the first half of the third century B.C. Down to this time sporadic translations had been done independently by Christians, Jews and recent converts to Islam. Beginning with al-Mamun and continuing under his immediate successors the work was centered mainly in the newly founded academy. The Abbasid era of translation lasted about a century after 750. Since most of the translators were Aramaic-speaking, many of the Greek works were first translated into Aramaic (Syriac) before their rendition into Arabic. Aramaic was the language Christ spoke.

The translators into Arabic did not interest themselves in Greek productions of the literary type. No close contact was established between the Arab mind and Greek drama, Greek poetry and Greek history. In that field Persian influence remained paramount. It was Greek philosophy, as originated by Plato and Aristotle and expounded by later Neo-Platonists, that served as the starting point of the voyage of intellectual discovery.

The sheikh of the translators, as the Arabs express it, was Hunayn ibn-Ishaq (Joannitius, 809-873), one of the greatest scholars and noblest characters of the age. Hunayn was a Nestorian Christian from al-Hirah, and as a youth acted as dispenser to a physician. Taking as a challenge a chiding remark by the master that the people of Hirah had no business with medicine and that he had better go and change money in the bazar, the lad left the service of his master in tears, but intent upon the study of Greek. Among other books in Arabic Hunayn is supposed to have prepared translations of Galen, Hippocrates and Dioscorides as well as of Plato's *Republic* and Aristotle's *Categories*, *Physics* and *Magna Moralia*. Among these his chief work was the rendition into Syriac and Arabic of almost all of Galen's scientific output. The seven books of Galen's anatomy, lost in the original Greek, have luckily been preserved in Arabic. Hunayn's Arabic version of the Old Testament from the Greek Septuagint did not survive.

Hunayn's ability as a translator is affirmed by the report that he and other translators received about 500 dinars (roughly $1,200) per month and that al-Mamun paid him in gold the weight of the books he translated. But he reached the summit of his glory not only as a translator but as a practitioner when he was appointed by the Caliph al-Mutawakkil as his private physician. His patron, however, once committed him to jail for a year for refusing the offer of rich rewards to concoct a poison for an enemy. When brought again before the caliph and threatened with death his reply was, "I have skill only in what is beneficial, and have studied naught else." Asked by the caliph, who then claimed that he was simply testing his physician's integrity, what prevented him from preparing the deadly poison, Hunayn replied:

"Two things: my religion and my profession. My religion decrees that we should do good even to our enemies, how much more to our friends.

119

And my profession is instituted for the benefit of humanity and limited to their relief and cure. Besides every physician is under oath never to give anyone a deadly medicine."

A modern French historian of medicine calls Hunayn "the greatest figure of the ninth century."

Before the age of translation was brought to an end practically all the extant works of Aristotle, many of which were of course spurious, had become accessible to the Arabic reader. All this took place while Europe was almost totally ignorant of Greek thought and science. For while al-Rashid and al-Mamun were delving into Greek and Persian philosophy their contemporaries in the West, Charlemagne and his lords, were reportedly dabbling in the art of writing their names. Aristotle's logical *Organon*, which in Arabic included Aristotle's *Rhetoric* and *Poetics* as well as Porphyry's *Isagoge*, soon took its place side by side with Arabic grammar as the basis of humanistic studies in Islam. This position it has maintained to the present day. Moslems accepted the idea of Neo-Platonic commentators that the teachings of Aristotle and Plato were substantially the same. Especially in Sufism, Moslem mysticism, did the influence of Neo-Platonism manifest itself. Through Arab scholars, particularly Avicenna and Averroës, as we shall later see, Platonism and Aristotelianism found their way into Latin and exercised a determining influence upon medieval European scholasticism.

This long and fruitful age of translation under

the early Abbasids was followed by one of original contribution which we shall discuss in a later chapter. Arabic, which in pre-Islamic days was only a language of poetry and after Muhammad mainly a language of revelation and religion, had become by the tenth century metamorphosed in a remarkable and unprecedented way into a pliant medium for expressing scientific thought and conveying philosophic ideas. In the meantime it had established itself as the language of diplomacy and polite intercourse from Central Asia, through the whole length of Northern Africa, to Spain. Since that time the peoples of Iraq, Syria and Palestine as well as of Egypt, Tunisia, Algeria and Morocco have expressed their best thought in the tongue of the Arabians.

The Life of the People

Arab historians had their interest too much centered in the caliph's affairs, in the tangled and bloody but to them all-important story of the rise and fall of dynasties and pretenders, and in the triumphs and mishaps of generals, viziers and the politically eminent of the day to leave us any adequate picture of the social and economic life of the common people. But from sporadic, incidental passages in their works, from literary sources and indeed from the facts of ordinary life in the little-changing Moslem Orient of today, it is possible to reconstruct an outline of that picture.

The woman of the ninth century enjoyed the same considerable measure of liberty as her sister in earlier years; but toward the end of the tenth century the system of strict seclusion and abso-

122

lute segregation of the sexes had become general. Not only do we read of women in the high circles of the early Abbasid period achieving distinction and exercising influence in state affairs, but of Arab maidens going to war and commanding troops, composing poetry and competing with men in literary pursuits or enlivening society with their wit, musical talent and vocal accomplishments.

In the period of decline, characterized by excessive concubinage, laxity of sex morality and indulgence in luxury, the position of woman sank to the low level we find in the *Arabian Nights*. There woman is represented as the personification of cunning and intrigue and as the repository of all base sentiments and unworthy thoughts.

Marriage has been regarded almost universally in Islam as a positive duty, the neglect of which is subject to severe reproach, and the gift of children, especially if sons, a boon from God. A wife's first duty consisted in the service of her husband, the care of the children and the management of household affairs; any spare time would be occupied with spinning and weaving.

Judging by the erotic expressions of the poets of the age, the early Arabian ideals of feminine beauty seem not to have undergone much change. The woman's stature should be like the bamboo among plants, her face as round as the full moon, her hair darker than the night, her cheeks white and rosy with a mole not unlike a drop of ambergris upon a plate of alabaster, her eyes intensely black and large like those of a wild deer, her eyelids drowsy or languid, her mouth small with teeth like pearls set in coral, her bosom pomegranate-like, her hips wide and her fingers tapering, the tips dyed with vermilion henna (from Arabic *hinna*).

The fashionable headdress for women was evidently a dome-shaped cap, round the bottom of which was a circlet that could be adorned with jewels. Among other objects of feminine adornment were anklets and bracelets. Men's clothing has varied but little since those days and the ancient style is still followed by the older generation in Lebanon and Syria. The common headgear was the black high-peaked hat, made of felt or wool. The wardrobe was completed by wide trousers of Persian origin, shirt, vest and jacket with outer mantle, the *jubbah*. This Arabic word has worked its way from Spanish, where we find it in a late tenth-century dictionary, into the rest of the Romance languages and thence into English and the other Germanic languages as well as the Slavonic. In English it has an interesting survival in "gibbet," meaning "gallows."

The most conspicuous piece of furniture in the home now came to be the *diwan*, a sofa extending along three sides of the room. Raised seats in the form of chairs were introduced under the earlier dynasty, but cushions laid on small square mattresses—a word derived from Arabic *matrah*—on the floor where one could comfortably squat remained popular. Handwoven carpets covered the floor. Food was served on large round trays of brass set on a low table in front of the *diwan* or the floor cushions. In the homes of the well-to-do the trays were of silver and the table of wood inlaid with ebony, mother-of-pearl or tortoise-shell—not unlike those still manufactured in Damascus. Those same people who had once enjoyed scorpions, beetles and weasels as a luxury, who thought rice a venomous food and used flattened bread for writing material, by this time had their gastronomic tastes whetted for the delicacies of the civilized world, including such Persian dishes as the greatly desired stew and the rich sweets. Their chickens were now fed on shelled nuts, almonds and milk. In summer, houses were cooled by ice. Nonalcoholic drinks in the form of sherbet, consisting of water sweetened with sugar and flavored with extracts of violets, bananas, roses or mulberries, were served. Coffee did not attain vogue until the fifteenth century, and tobacco was unknown before the discovery of the New World. A ninth- to tenth-century author has left us a work intended to give an exposition of the sentiments and manners of a man of culture, a gentleman, in that period. He is one in possession of polite behavior, manly honor and elegant manners, who abstains from joking, holds fellowship with the right comrades, has high standards of veracity, is scrupulous in the fulfillment of his promises, keeps a secret, wears unsoiled and unpatched clothes, and at the table takes small mouthfuls, converses or laughs but little, chews his food slowly, does not lick his fingers, avoids garlic and onions and refrains from using the toothpick in toilet rooms, baths, public meetings and on the streets.

Alcoholic drinks were often indulged in both in company and in private. Judging by the countless stories of revelry in such works as the *Aghani* and the *Arabian Nights*, and by the numerous songs and poems in praise of wine, prohibition, one of the distinctive features of the Moslem religion, prohibited no more than did the eighteenth amendment to the Constitution of the United States. Even caliphs, viziers, princes and judges paid no heed to the religious injunction. *Khamr*, made of dates, was the favorite beverage.

Convivial parties featuring "the daughter of the vine" and song were not uncommon. At these drinking bouts the hosts and guests perfumed their beards with civet or rose water and wore special garments of bright colors. The room was made fragrant by ambergris or aloeswood burning in a censer. The songstresses who participated in such gatherings were mostly slaves of loose character, as illustrated by many stories; they constituted the gravest menace to the morals of the youth of the age. The laity had access to wine in the Christian monasteries and the special bars conducted mainly by Jews. Christians and Jews were the "bootleggers" of the time.

"Cleanliness is a part of faith"—so runs a Prophetic tradition that is still on every lip in Moslem lands. Arabia had no baths that we

hear of before Muhammad. He himself is represented as prejudiced against them and as having
permitted men to enter them for purposes of
cleanliness only, each wearing a cloth. In the
time we are studying, however, public baths had
become popular not only for ceremonial ablu-
tions and for their salutary effects, but also as re-
sorts of amusement and mere luxury. Women
were allowed their use on specially reserved
days. At the beginning of the tenth century
Baghdad boasted some 27,000 public baths, and
in other times even 60,000, all of which—like
most figures in Arabic sources—seem highly exaggerated. A Moorish traveler who visited Baghdad in 1327 found in each of the thirteen quarters
composing its west side two or three baths of the
most elaborate kind each supplied with hot and
cold running water.

Then as now the bathhouse comprised several
chambers with mosaic pavements and marble-
lined inner walls clustering round a large central chamber. This innermost chamber, crowned
by a dome studded with small round glazed aper-
tures for the admission of light, was heated by
steam rising from a central jet of water in the
middle of a basin. The outer rooms were used
for lounging and for enjoying drinks and re-
freshments.

Sports, like the fine arts, have throughout history been characteristic more of Indo-European
than of Semitic civilization. Engaging in them
involves physical exertion for its own sake, a
rather absurd idea to the son of Arabia with his

127

poetical temperament and his well-founded respect for the heat of the daylight hours.

In the list of outdoor sports, however, were archery, polo, ball and mallets (a sort of croquet or hockey), fencing, javelin-throwing, horse racing, and above all hunting. Among the qualifications of a prospective boon companion, writers list ability in archery, hunting, playing ball and chess—in all of which the companion may equal his royal master with no fear of affronting him. Among the caliphs particularly fond of polo was al-Mutasim, whose Turkish general once refused a play against him because he did not want to be against the commander of the believers even in a game. Interesting references are also made to a ball game in which a broad piece of wood was used. Could this be tennis in its rudimentary form? The word "tennis," generally supposed to have come from the French verb *tenez,* meaning "take heed," is probably from *Tinnis,* the Arabic name of an Egyptian city in the Delta noted in the Middle Ages for its linen fabrics, which may have been used for making tennis balls.

The number of early Arabic books dealing with hunting, trapping and falconry testify to the keen interest in these sports. Falconry and hawking were introduced into Arabia from Persia, as the Arabic vocabulary relating to these sports indicates. They became particularly favored in the later period of the caliphate and in that of the Crusades. Hunting with the falcon or sparrow hawk is still practiced in Persia, Iraq and Syria in practically the same manner as described in the *Arabian Nights*. Incidentally, the first thing a Moslem hunter must do after seizing his prey is to cut its throat; otherwise its flesh would be unlawful.

At the head of the social register stood the caliph and his family, the government officials and the satellites of these groups. In this last class we may include the soldiers and bodyguards, the favored friends and boon companions, as well as the "clients" and servants.

The servants were almost all slaves recruited from non-Moslem peoples and captured by force, taken prisoner in time of war or purchased in time of peace. Some were negroes, others were Turks, and still others were white. The white slaves were mainly Greeks and Slavs, Armenians and Berbers. Some were eunuchs attached to the service of the harem, others, termed *ghilman*, who might also be eunuchs, were the recipients of special favors from their masters, wore rich and attractive uniforms and often beautified and perfumed their bodies in effeminate fashion. We read of *ghilman* in the reign of al-Rashid; but it was evidently the Caliph al-Amin who, following Persian precedent, established in the Arabic world the *ghilman* institution for the practice of unnatural sexual relations. A judge of whom there is record used four hundred such youths. Poets did not disdain to give public expression to their perverted passions and to address amorous pieces of their compositions to "beardless young boys."

The maidens among slaves were also used as

singers, dancers and concubines, and some of them exerted appreciable influence over their caliph masters. Such was "she of the mole," whom al-Rashid had bought for 70,000 dirhams and in a fit of jealousy bestowed on one of his male servants. In order to win him from another singing-girl to whom he became attached, al-Rashid's wife Zubaydah presented her husband with ten maidens, two of whom became the mothers of caliphs. The legendary story of Towaddud, the beautiful and talented slave girl in *The Thousand and One Nights*, whom al-Rashid was willing to purchase for 100,000 dinars after she had passed with flying colors a searching test before his savants in medicine, law, astronomy, philosophy, music and mathematics —to say nothing of rhetoric, grammar, poetry, history and the Koran—illustrates how highly cultured some of these maids must have been. Al-Amin's contribution consisted in organizing a corps of female pages, the members of which bobbed their hair, dressed like boys and wore silk turbans. The innovation soon became popular with both the higher and the lower classes of society. An eyewitness reports that when on a Palm Sunday he called on al-Mamun he found in his presence twenty Greek maidens, all bedecked and adorned, dancing with gold crosses on their necks and olive branches and palm leaves in their hands. The distribution of 3,000 dinars among the dancers brought the affair to a grand finale.

Al-Mutawakkil, according to a report, had 4,000 concubines, all of whom (we are asked to believe) shared his nuptial bed. It was customary for governors and generals to send presents, including girls received or exacted from among their subjects, to the caliph or vizir; failure to do so was interpreted as a sign of rebellion.

The commonalty was composed of an upper class bordering on the aristocracy and comprised litterateurs, learned men, artists, merchants, craftsmen and professionals; and of a lower class forming the majority of the nation and made up of farmers, herdsmen and country folk who represented the native population and now enjoyed the status of dhimmis.

The wide extent of the empire and the high level which civilization attained necessitated extensive international trade. The early merchants were Christians, Jews and Zoroastrians, but they were later largely superseded by Moslems and Arabs, who did not disdain trade as they did agriculture. Such ports as Baghdad, Basrah, Siraf, Cairo and Alexandria soon developed into centers of active land and maritime commerce.

Eastward, Moslem traders ventured as far as China. This trade was based on silk, the earliest of China's magnificent gifts to the West, and usually followed what has been styled "the great silk way" going through Samarqand and Chinese Turkestan, a region less traversed today by civilized men than almost any other part of the habitable world. Goods were generally transported by relays; few caravans went the whole distance. Sea traders carried Islam into the island, which in 1949 formed the Republic of Indonesia.

The Arabs

Westward, Moslem merchants reached Morocco and Spain. A thousand years before de Lesseps an Arab caliph, Harun, entertained the idea of digging a canal through the Isthmus of Suez. Arab Mediterranean trade, however, never rose to great prominence. The Black Sea was likewise inhospitable to it, though in the tenth century brisk land trade took place with the peoples of the Volga regions to the north. But the Caspian Sea, because of its proximity to the Persian centers and the prosperous cities of Samarqand and Bukhara with their hinterland, was the scene of active commercial intercourse. Moslem merchants carried with them dates, sugar, cotton and woolen fabrics, steel tools and glassware; they imported among other commodities, spices, camphor and silk from farther Asia, and ivory, ebony and negro slaves from Africa.

An idea of the fortunes amassed by the Rothschilds and Rockefellers of the age may be gained from the case of the Baghdad jeweler ibn-al-Jassas, who remained wealthy after a caliph had confiscated 16,000,000 dinars of his property, became the first of a family of distinguished jewel merchants. Certain Basrah merchants whose ships carried goods to distant parts of the world had an annual income of more than a million dirhams each. An uneducated miller of Basrah and Baghdad could afford to distribute a hundred dinars as daily alms among the poor. In Siraf the home of the average merchant cost over ten thousand dinars, some over thirty thousand dinars; and many maritime traders were worth

4,000,000 dinars each. A dinar was the equivalent of about $2.40.

No commercial activity could have reached such dimensions had it not rested on extensive home industry and agriculture. Hand industry flourished in various parts of the empire. In Western Asia it centered chiefly in the manufacture of rugs, tapestry, silk, cotton and woolen fabrics, satin, brocade, sofas (from *suffah*) and cushion covers, as well as other articles of furniture and kitchen utensils. The many looms of Persia and Iraq turned out carpets and textiles maintained at a high standard by distinctive marks. One caliph's mother had a rug specially ordered for her at a cost of 130,000,000 dirhams; it bore figures of all sorts of birds in gold, with rubies and other precious stones for eyes. A quarter in Baghdad named after Attab, an Umayyad prince who was its most distinguished resident, gave its name to a striped fabric, *attabi*, first manufactured there in the twelfth century. The fabric was imitated by the Arabs in Spain and under the trade name *tabi* became popular in France, Italy and other lands of Europe. The term survives in "tabby," applied to streaked or marked cats. Kufah produced the silk and partly silk kerchiefs for the head that are still worn under the name *kufiyah*.

In ancient Susiana were a number of factories famous for the embroidery of damask (a fabric originally made in Damascus) figured with gold, and for curtains made of spun silk. Their camel- and goat-hair fabrics, as well as their spun-silk cloaks, were widely known. Shiraz yielded striped woolen cloaks, also gauzes and brocades. Under the name of "taffeta" European ladies of the Middle Ages bought in their native shops the Persian silken cloth *taftah*.

The glass of Sidon, Tyre, and other Lebanese and Syrian towns, a survival of the ancient Phoenician industry which next to the Egyptian was the oldest glass industry in history, was proverbial for its clarity and thinness. As a result of the Crusades, Syrian glass became the forerunner of the stained glass in the cathedrals of Europe. Glass and metal vases of Syrian workmanship were in great demand as articles of utility and luxury.

Worthy of special note is the manufacture of writing paper, introduced in the middle of the eighth century into Samarqand from China. The paper of Samarqand, which, as we have noted, was captured by the Moslems in 704, was considered matchless. Before the close of that century Baghdad saw its first paper mill. Gradually other mills for making paper followed: Egypt had its factory about 900 or earlier, Morocco about 1100, Spain about 1150; and various kinds of paper, white and colored, were produced. From Moslem Spain and from Italy, in the twelfth and thirteenth centuries, the manufacture of paper, as we shall see later, finally worked its way into Christian Europe, where, with the later discovery of printing from movable type, 1450-1455, it made possible the measure of popular education which Europe and America now enjoy.

Agriculture received great impetus under the early Abbasids because their capital itself lay in a most favored spot, an alluvial plain; because they realized that farming was the chief source of the state income; and because the tilling of the land was almost wholly in the hands of the native inhabitants, whose status was somewhat improved under the new regime. Deserted farms and ruined villages in different parts of the empire were gradually rehabilitated. The lower region of the Tigris-Euphrates valley, the richest, with the exception of Egypt, in the whole empire and the traditional site of the garden of Eden, was the object of special attention on the part of the central government. Canals from the Euphrates formed a "veritable network." Arab geographers speak of caliphs "digging" or "opening" "rivers," when in most cases the process involved was one of redigging or reopening canals that had existed since Babylonian days. In Iraq as well as Egypt the task consisted mainly in keeping the ancient systems in order. Even before World War I, when the Ottoman government commissioned Sir William Willcocks to study the irrigation problem of Iraq, his report stressed the necessity of clearing the old watercourses rather than of constructing new ones. It should be noted, however, that the face of this great alluvial plain has greatly changed since Abbasid days and that both the Tigris and the

Euphrates have considerably shifted their courses.

Most of the fruit trees and vegetables grown at present in Western Asia were known at this time, with the exception of mangoes, potatoes, tomatoes and similar plants introduced in recent times from the New World and distant European colonies. The orange tree, allied to the citron and lemon, had its native habitat in northern India or Malays, whence it spread into Western Asia, the adjoining lands of the Mediterranean basin and eventually through the Arabs in Spain into Europe. The sugar-cane plantations of southwestern Persia, with their noted refineries, were about this time followed by similar ones on the Syrian coast, from which place the Crusaders later introduced the cane and the sugar into Europe. Thus did this sweet commodity, probably of Bengalese origin, which has since become an indispensable ingredient in the daily food of civilized man, work its way westward.

The agricultural class, who constituted the bulk of the population of the empire and its chief source of revenue, were the original inhabitants of the land, now reduced to the position of dhimmis—those with whom a compact for religious tolerance had been made. The Arab considered it below his dignity to engage in agricultural pursuits. Originally "Scripturaries,"—Christians, Jews and Sabians—the dhimmis had their status widened to include certain other sects. In country places and on their farms these dhimmis clung to their ancient cultural patterns and preserved their native languages. The compact was observed well, on the whole, although there were periods of religious persecution.

In cities Christians and Jews held important financial, clerical and professional positions. This of course led to jealousy on the part of the Moslem populace and found expression in official enactments, but most of this discriminating legislation remained "ink on paper" and was not consistently enforced.

The pious Umayyad Caliph Umar II ordered Christians and Jews to don distinctive dress, and he excluded them from public offices. Harun al-Rashid was evidently the first to reenact some of the old measures. The Caliph al-Mutawakkil in 850 and 854 decreed that Christians and Jews should affix wooden images of devils to their houses, level their graves even with the ground, wear outer garments of honey color, i.e. yellow, put two honey-colored patches on the clothes of their slaves, one sewn on the back and the other on the front, and ride only on mules and asses with wooden saddles marked by two pomegranate-like balls on the cantle. It was on account of this distinctive dress that the dhimmi acquired the epithet "spotted." One other grave disability under which the dhimmis labored was a ruling of the Moslem jurists of the period that the testimony of a Christian or a Jew could not be accepted against a Moslem; for the Jews and Christians had once corrupted the text of their scripture, as the Koran charges, and therefore could no more be trusted. But in spite of these restrictions the Christians under the caliphs enjoyed a

The Arabs

large measure of toleration. We even read of
Christian vizirs in the latter half of the ninth
century, and such Christian high officials received the usual marks of honor, for we find
record of certain Moslems objecting to kissing
their hands. One of the most remarkable features
of Christianity under the caliphs was its possession of enough vitality to make it an aggressive
church, sending its missionaries as far as India
and China.

As one of the "protected" peoples the Jews
fared on the whole even better than the Christians, and that in spite of several unfavorable
references in the Koran. Under several caliphs
we read of more than one Jew assuming responsible state positions. In Baghdad itself the Jews
maintained a good-sized colony which continued to flourish until the fall of the city. Benjamin
of Tudela, a rabbi who visited the colony about
1170, found it in possession of ten rabbinical
schools and twenty-three synagogues; the principal one, adorned with variegated marble, was
richly ornamented with gold and silver. Benjamin tells in glowing terms the high esteem in
which the chief rabbi was held as a descendant
of David and head of the community of all Jews
owing allegiance to the Baghdad caliphate. On
his way to an audience with the caliph he appeared dressed in embroidered silk, wore a white
turban gleaming with gems and was accompanied
by a retinue of horsemen. Ahead of him marched
a herald calling out: "Make way before our lord
the son of David!"

The Life of the People

This is the panorama of the life of the people of the caliphate and their relationships to one another. We are now in the third stage of the Arab conquest. The first, as we have seen, was military and political—the march of Arab arms. The second was religious, beginning with the first century of Abbasid rule. During this period the bulk of the population of the empire was converted to Islam. The third stage was linguistic: the victory of the Arabic tongue over the native languages of the subjugated peoples. This was the slowest and the one in which the conquered presented the greatest resistance. Apparently men are more ready to give up their political and even religious loyalties than their linguistic ones.

Arabic as the language of learning won its day before Arabic as the vernacular. In the preceding chapter we saw how fresh streams of thought from Greek culture, Persia and India resulted in the beginnings of a new culture in the 800's in Baghdad. Now, Arabic has triumphed as the vehicle of Arab civilization. This ushers in Islam's intellectual golden age.

Science and Literature

We have reached the period in which the Arabic language became the vehicle for fresh and original work in science, especially in medicine, astronomy, alchemy (which was the beginning of the science of chemistry) and geography, in mathematics—and also in philosophy, history, ethics and literature. The period begins in the latter half of the ninth century, following the epoch of translation which lasted roughly a hundred years, from 750 to 850. It is characterized by a galaxy of names, few familiar to general public in the West today though many of them well known and esteemed by modern students in the arts and the sciences. We shall be able to mention only a few, representatives of Islam's great contributors to the civilization which we know.

140

By now the Arabs had not only assimilated the ancient lore of Persia and the classical heritage of Greece, but had adapted both to their own peculiar needs and ways of thinking. Their translations, modified by the Arab mind in the course of several centuries, were passed on, together with many new contributions, to Europe through Syria, Spain and Sicily and laid the basis of that canon of knowledge which dominated medieval European thought. And transmission, from the standpoint of the history of culture, is no less essential than origination, for had the researches of Aristotle, Galen and Ptolemy been lost to posterity the world would have been as poor as if they had never been produced. The line of demarcation between translated and original work is, of course, not always clearly drawn. Many of the translators were also contributors.

Arab interest in the curative science found expression in the Prophetic tradition that made science twofold: theology and medicine. The physician was at the same time metaphysician, philosopher and sage. In the curative use of drugs some remarkable advances were made at this time by the Arabs. It was they who established the first apothecary shops, founded the earliest school of pharmacy and produced the first pharmacopoeia. As early as the days of the Caliph al-Mamun pharmacists had to pass an examination. Like druggists, physicians also were required to submit to a test. Following a case of malpractice a distinguished physician was ordered by the

141

caliph in 931 to examine all practicing physicians and grant certificates only to those who satisfied the requirements. Over eight hundred and sixty such men in Baghdad passed the test and the capital rid itself of its quacks. Something like a rural health service was organized when, on the orders of a vizir, a staff of physicians was sent from place to place carrying drugs and administering relief to ailing people. Other physicians made daily visits to jails. Such facts show an intelligent interest in public hygiene unkown to the rest of the world at that time. The first hospital in Islam was established by Harun al-Rashid at the beginning of the ninth century, following the Persian model. Not long afterward other hospitals to the number of thirty-four grew up throughout the Moslem world. Cairo saw its first hospital about 872, an institution which survived until the fifteenth century. Traveling clinics made their appearance in the eleventh century. Moslem hospitals had special wards for women and each had its own dispensary. Some were equipped with medical libraries and offered courses in medicine.

The most notable medical authors who followed the epoch of the great translators were Persian in nationality but Arab in language. The portraits of two of these, Rhazes and Avicenna, adorn the great hall of the School of Medicine at the University of Paris.

Rhazes (al-Razi), who lived from 865 to 925, was one of the keenest original thinkers and greatest clinicians not only of Islam but of the

Middle Ages. In selecting a new site for the great hospital at Baghdad, of which he was chief physician, he is said to have hung up shreds of meat in different places, choosing the spot where they showed the least signs of putrefaction. He is considered the inventor of the seton in surgery. One of his principal works on alchemy, the *Book of Secrets*, after having passed through numerous editorial hands was rendered into Latin in the late twelfth century by the eminent translator Gerard of Cremona and became a chief source of chemical knowledge until the fourteenth century. Under the title *De spiritibus et corporibus* it was quoted by Roger Bacon. The best-known monograph of Rhazes is a treatise on smallpox and measles, the earliest of its kind and rightly considered an ornament to the medical literature of the Arabs. His most important work, however, was *al-Hawi*, a comprehensive book, first translated into Latin under the auspices of Charles I of Anjou by the Sicilian Jewish physician Faraj ben-Salim in 1279. Under the title *Continens* it was repeatedly printed from 1486 onwards, a fifth edition appearing in Venice in 1542. As the name indicates, this book was meant to be encyclopedic in its range of medical information. It sums up the knowledge the Arabs possessed at that time of Greek, Persian and Hindu medicine and adds some fresh contributions. Printed when printing was still in its infancy, these medical works of Rhazes exercised for centuries a remarkable influence over the minds of the Latin West.

The Arabs

The most illustrious name in Arabic medical annals after Rhazes is Avicenna (ibn-Sina). His encyclopedic treatise, translated as the *Canon*, worked its way into a position of preeminence in the medical literature of the age, becoming the textbook for medical education in the schools of Europe. In the last thirty years of the fifteenth century it passed through fifteen Latin editions and one Hebrew. In recent years a partial translation into English has been made. Its materia medica considers some seven hundred and sixty drugs. From the twelfth to the seventeenth centuries this work served as the chief guide to medical science in the West and is still in occasional use in the Moslem East. In the words of Dr. William Osler it has remained "a medical bible for a longer period than any other work."

In the field of philosophy the primary contribution of the Arabs—and it was a highly significant one—was the bringing of Greek thought into harmony with the ideas of Islam. To the Arabs philosophy was a knowledge of the true cause of things as they really are, in so far as it is possible to ascertain them by human faculties. They adapted this essentially Greek point of view, modified by the thought of the conquered peoples and by other Eastern influences, to the mental proclivities of Islam and expressed it through the medium of Arabic. As students of Greek they considered Aristotle's works the complete codification of philosophical lore, and Galen's the summation of medical lore. Greek philosophy and medicine meant then, of course, all that the West possessed. As Moslems the Arabs believed that the Koran and Islamic theology were the summations of religious law and experience. Their original contribution, therefore, was made in the borderland between philosophy and religion on one hand and philosophy and medicine on the other. It is to the eternal glory of medieval Islam that it succeeded for the first time in the history of human thought in harmonizing and reconciling monotheism—the idea of a single God and the greatest contribution of the ancient Semitic world—with Greek philosophy, the greatest contribution of the ancient Indo-European world. Islam thus led Christian Europe toward the modern point of view.

Learning in the ancient and medieval world—in the world of Islam especially—was far less compartmented than we are accustomed to consider it today. Philosophers could be mathematicians and musicians, astronomers could be poets. The modern Western reader will, for example, be greatly surprised to find under the roll of Islam's most distinguished astronomers the celebrated name of Umar al-Khayyam—the author of the even more celebrated *Rubaiyat*. He was indeed a Persian poet and a freethinker; he was also a first-class mathematician and astronomer. The work of al-Kindi is also typical. As philosopher he endeavored in Neo-Platonic fashion to combine the views of Plato and Aristotle and regarded Neo-Pythagorean mathematics as the basis of all science. But he was more than a philosopher; he was an astrologer, alchemist, optician

145

and musical theorist. No less than two hundred and sixty-five works are ascribed to him, but unhappily most of them have been lost. His principal work on optics, based on the *Optics* of Euclid, was widely used in both East and West and influenced Roger Bacon. His works on music indicate that measured song, or mensural music, was known to the Moslems centuries before it was introduced into Christian Europe.

The scientific study of astronomy in Islam was begun under the influence of an Indian work, the *Siddhanta*, brought to Baghdad in 771. Early in the ninth century the first regular observations with fairly accurate instruments were made in southwest Persia and before the middle of that century the Caliph al-Mamun erected astronomical observatories in Baghdad and outside Damascus. The equipment in those days consisted of quadrant, astrolabe, dial and globe. This caliph's astronomers performed one of the most delicate geodetic operations—the measuring of the length of a terrestrial degree. The object was to determine the size of the earth and its circumference on the assumption that the earth was round. The measurement, carried out on the plain north of the Euphrates and also near Palmyra, yielded 56⅔ Arabic miles as the length of a degree of the meridian—a remarkably accurate result, exceeding the real length of the degree at that place only by about 2,877 feet.

Among the astronomers who possibly took part in this operation was al-Khwarizmi, one of the greatest scientific minds of Islam and the man who influenced mathematical thought to a greater degree than any other medieval writer. Apart from compiling the oldest astronomical tables, al-Khwarizmi composed the oldest work on arithmetic and the oldest work on algebra, which was translated into Latin and used until the sixteenth century as the principal mathematical textbook of European universities and served to introduce into Europe the science of algebra, and with it the name. His works were also responsible for the introduction into the West of the Arabic numerals, called "algorisms" after him. Zero or cipher (Arabic *sifr*) was also then introduced.

After materia medica, astronomy and mathematics, the Arabs made their greatest scientific contribution in chemistry. In the study of chemistry and other physical sciences they introduced the objective experiment, a decided improvement over the hazy speculation of the Greeks. Accurate in the observation of phenomena and diligent in the accumulation of facts, the Arabs nevertheless found it difficult to project proper hypotheses and draw truly scientific conclusions. The final elaboration of a system was their weakest point.

The father of Arabic alchemy (the word goes back from Arabic through Greek to an ancient Egyptian word meaning "black") was Geber (Jabir ibn-Hayyan), who flourished in Kufah about 776. Like his Egyptian and Greek forerunners, Geber acted on the assumption that base metals such as tin, lead, iron and copper could

147

be transmuted into gold or silver by means of a mysterious substance, and to this search he devoted his energy. He more clearly recognized and stated the importance of experimentation than any other early alchemist and made noteworthy advance in both the theory and practice of chemistry. Western tradition credits him with the discovery of several chemical compounds not mentioned in the twenty-two surviving Arab works that bear his name. It is evident that the vast majority of the hundred extant alchemical works in Arabic and in Latin which pass under his name are spurious. Nevertheless, the works to which his name was attached were after the fourteenth century the most influential chemical treatises in both Europe and Asia. Of a few contributions we are certain. Geber described scientifically the two important chemical operations of calcination and reduction. He improved on the methods for evaporation, sublimation, melting and crystallization. The claim that he knew how to prepare crude sulphuric and nitric acids and mix them so as to produce aqua regia, in which gold and silver could be dissolved, is unsubstantiated. In general he modified the Aristotelian theory of the constituents of metal in a way that survived, with slight alterations, until the beginning of modern chemistry in the eighteenth century.

The institution of the holy pilgrimage, the orientation of the mosques toward Mecca and the need for determining the direction of the Kaaba at the time of prayer gave religious impetus to the Moslem study of geography. Astrology, which necessitated the determining of the latitudes and longitudes of all places throughout the world, added its scientific influence. Moslem traders between the seventh and ninth centuries reached China on the east both by sea and by land, attained the island of Zanzibar and the farthest coasts of Africa on the south, penetrated Russia on the north and were checked in their advance westward only by the dreaded waters of the "Sea of Darkness"—the Atlantic. The reports of returning merchants naturally aroused popular interest in distant lands and alien peoples. Ptolemy's *Geography* was translated into Arabic either directly or through Syriac several times, and with this as a model the famous Khwarizmi constructed an "image of the earth," a map executed by him and sixty-nine other scholars— the first map of the heavens and the world in Islam. The early Arab geographers had gained from India the notion that there was a world center which they styled *arin*, a corruption of the name of an Indian town in Ptolemy's *Geography*, where there had been an astronomical observatory and on the meridian of which the "world cupola" or "summit" was supposed to lie. This they located on the equator between the extremes of east and west. The western prime meridian was thought by them to be 90° from this mythical place. Moslem geographers in general measured longitude from the prime meridian used by Ptolemy, that of the islands now called the Canaries.

Whereas in philosophy and medicine the Greek influence was paramount, in historical and literary compositions, to which we now come, the Persian example was followed. The form of presentation, however, continued to be that of the stereotyped Islamic tradition. Each event is related in the words of eyewitnesses or contemporaries and transmitted to the final narrator, the author, through a chain of intermediary reporters. This technique served to develop exactitude, as did also the insistence on dating occurrences even to the month and day. But the authenticity of the reported facts generally depended upon the continuity of this chain and the confidence in the integrity of each reporter rather than upon a critical examination of the fact itself. Apart from the use of personal judgment in the choice of the series of authorities and in the arrangement of the data, the historian exercised very little power of analysis, criticism, comparison or inference.

Although Arab historians wrote copiously of the events of the time, the product most characteristic of the Arab approach to history is the *hadith*, or science of religious tradition. In the course of the first two and a half centuries after Muhammad the records of his sayings and doings increased in number and copiousness. Whenever an issue—religious, political or sociological—arose each party sought to find authority for its views in some word or decision of the Prophet, be it real or fictitious.

Every perfect hadith consists of two parts:

a chain of authorities and a text. The text follows the chain and should be in direct address: "A related to me that B related to him, on the authority of C, on the authority of D, on the authority of E, who said . . ." The same formula was used in historiography and in "wisdom literature." In all these fields criticism was usually external, being limited to a consideration of the reputation of the transmitters, who were at the same time guarantors, and to the possibility of their forming an uninterrupted chain leading back to the Prophet.

After the Romans the Arabs were the only medieval people who cultivated the science of jurisprudence and evolved an independent system. It was primarily based on the Koran and the hadith and influenced by the Greco-Roman system. Through the canon law of Islam the totality of Allah's commandments as revealed in the Koran and elaborated in the hadith was communicated to later generations.

The prescriptions of the canon law regulate for the Moslem his entire life in its religious, political and social aspects. They govern his marital and civic relations as well as his relations with non-Moslems. Ethical conduct derives its sanctions and inhibitions from the sacred law. All man's acts are classified under five legal categories: (1) what is considered absolute duty, embracing actions the commission of which is rewarded and the omission punished by law; (2) commendable or meritorious actions, the performance of which is rewarded but the omission

151

not punished; (3) permissible actions, which are legally indifferent; (4) reprehensible actions, which are disapproved but not punishable; (5) forbidden actions, the doing of which calls for punishment.

Ethical works based on the Koran and tradition, though numerous, do not exhaust all the material in Arabic literature dealing with morals. In all these Moslem philosophies, the virtues of resignation, contentment and endurance are admired; vices are treated as maladies of the soul with the moral philosopher as the physician; and the classification is founded on the analysis of the faculties of the soul, each faculty having its own virtue and its own vice.

Arabic literature in the narrow sense of *adab,* or belles-lettres, which reached its height around the year 1000, tended to be affected and ornate, in response to Persian influence. The terse, incisive and simple expression of early days had gone forever. It was supplanted by a polished and elegant style, rich in elaborate similes and replete with rhymes. Of the literature of the period, the West has picked out one book on which to center its attention—*Alf Laylah wa-Laylah*—"A Thousand and One Nights," better known as the *Arabian Nights.* The first draft, made by al-Jahshiyari (d. 942), was from an old Persian tale. Other tales, and the name of the heroine, Scheherazade, were added by local story-tellers. As time went on additions were made from numberless sources—Indian, Greek, Hebrew, Egyptian, Oriental folktales of every description.

152

The fabulous court of Harun al-Rashid provided a large number of humorous anecdotes and love stories. The final compilation of the *Nights* was not made until the fourteenth century. It is, incidentally, far more popular in the West than in the East.

When the *Arabian Nights* had been put into final form in Arabic the golden age of Moslem scientific and literary progress had of course ended. In no branch of pure or physical science was any appreciable advance made after Abbasid days. The Moslems of today, if dependent on their own books, would indeed have less than their distant ancestors in the eleventh century. In medicine, philosophy, mathematics, botany and other disciplines a certain point was reached —and the mind of Islam seemed to stand still. Reverence for the past and its traditions, both religious and scientific, bound the Arab intellect with fetters which it is only now beginning to shake off.

The Fine Arts

In his art as in his poetry the Arab, a Semite, showed a keen appreciation of the particular and the subjective, with a delicate sense for detail but no particular capacity for harmonizing the various parts into a great and united whole. However, in architecture and painting particularly, he did not, as he had in the sciences, attain a certain degree of progress and then make no further advancement.

Of the architectural monuments which once adorned the city of Baghdad no trace has been left. Two of the noblest surviving structures of Islam, the Umayyad Mosque at Damascus and the Dome of the Rock at Jerusalem, date from the earlier period, as we have noted. That there was great splendor we know, but so complete was the destruction wrought by a civil war be-

154

tween the caliphs al-Amin and al-Mamun, by the final devastation of the capital by the Mongols in 1258 and by natural causes, that even the sites of most of these palaces cannot today be identified.

Outside of the capital no Abbasid ruin can be dated with any degree of probability prior to the reign of al-Mutawakkil (847-861), the builder of the great mosque at Samarra. This congregational mosque, which cost 700,000 dinars, was rectangular and the multifoil arches of its windows suggest Indian influence. Such Abbasid remains as have survived at Raqqah, of the late eighth century, and at Samarra carry on the tradition of Asiatic, more particularly Persian, architecture in contrast to the Umayyad structures, which bear clear traces of Byzantine-Syrian art.

The Moslem theologians were hostile to all forms of representational art, which the Koran forbade, but their disapproval no more stopped its development along Islamic lines than did the more explicit koranic injunction against wine enforce prohibition in Moslem society. We have already noticed that one caliph set upon the dome of his palace the figure of a horseman which might have served as a weathercock, that another had his pleasure boats on the Tigris fashioned like lions, eagles and dolphins, and that still another had a gold and silver tree with eighteen branches planted in a huge tank in his palace. On either side of the tank stood the statues of fifteen horsemen, dressed in brocade and armed with lances, constantly moving as though in combat.

The builder of Samarra, the Caliph al-Mutasim, had the walls of his palace there ornamented with frescoes of nude female figures and hunting scenes, probably the work of Christian artists. His second successor, al-Mutawakkil, under whom this temporary capital reached its zenith, employed for the mural decoration of his palace Byzantine painters who had no scruples against including among the many pictures a church with monks.

In Islam painting was pressed into the service of religion at a rather late date and never became its handmaid as it did in Buddhism and Christianity. The earliest record of any pictorial representation of the Prophet was noted by an Arabian traveler of the late ninth century who saw it in the Chinese court, but it may well have been produced by Nestorian Christians. Moslem religious painting does not make its full appearance until the beginning of the fourteenth century. Its derivation was evidently from the art of the Oriental Christian churches, particularly the Jacobite and the Nestorian, and developed from book decoration.

Since early antiquity the Persians, whose culture the Arabs appropriated, had proved themselves masters of decorative design and color. Through their efforts the industrial arts of Islam attained a high degree of excellence. Carpet weaving, as old as Pharaonic Egypt, was especially developed. Hunting and garden scenes

156

were favored in rug designs, and alum was used in the dye to render the many colors fast. Decorated silk fabrics, the product of Moslem hand looms in Egypt and Syria, were so highly prized in Europe that Crusaders and other Westerners chose them above all textiles as wrappings for relics and saints.

In ceramics, another art as ancient as Egypt and Susa, the reproduction of the human form and of animals and plants, as well as geometric and epigraphic figures, attained a beauty of decorative style unsurpassed in any other Moslem art. Qashani tile, decorated with conventional flowers, which was introduced from Persia to Damascus, found great vogue, together with mosaic work, in exterior and interior decoration of buildings. Better than any others, the characters of the Arabic alphabet lent themselves to decorative designs and became a powerful motif in Islamic art. They even became religious symbols. Particularly in Antoich, Aleppo, Damascus and such ancient Phoenician towns as Tyre were the processes of enameling and gilding glass perfected. Among the treasures of the Louvre, the British Museum and the Arab Museum of Cairo are exquisite pieces from Samarra and Fustat, including plates, cups, vases, ewers and lamps for home and mosque use, painted with brilliant lusters and acquiring through the ages metallic glazes of changing rainbow hue.

The art of calligraphy, which drew its prestige from its aim to perpetuate the word of God, and enjoyed the approval of the Koran, arose in the second or third Moslem century and soon became the most highly prized art. It was entirely Islamic and its influence on painting was appreciable. Through it the Moslem sought a channel for his esthetic nature, which could not express itself through the representation of animate objects. The calligrapher held a position of dignity and honor far above the painter. Even rulers sought to win religious merit by copying the Koran. Arabic books of history and literature have preserved for us with honorable mention the names of several calligraphers, but kept their silence in the case of architects, painters and metalworkers. Calligraphy is perhaps the only Arab art which today has Christian and Moslem representatives in Constantinople, Cairo, Beirut and Damascus whose productions excel in elegance and beauty any masterpieces that the ancients ever produced.

Not only calligraphy but its associate arts—color decoration, illumination, and the whole craft of bookbinding—owed their genesis and development to their relation to the sacred book. Under the late Abbasids began the art of book decoration and Koran illumination which reached its highest development in the fifteenth century.

The legists' disapproval of music was no more effective in Baghdad than it had been before in Damascus. The refined and dazzling court of Harun al-Rashid patronized music and singing, as it did science and art, to the extent of becoming the center of a galaxy of musical stars.

The Fine Arts

Salaried musicians accompanied by men and women slave singers thrived in it and furnished the theme for numberless fantastic anecdotes immortalized in the pages of the *Arabian Nights*. Two thousand such singers took part in a musical festival under the caliph's patronage. His son al-Amin held a similar night entertainment in which the personnel of the palace, both male and female, danced till dawn.

Typical of the singers of the day was a protégé of Harun al-Rashid called Mukhariq, a slave who when young had been bought by a woman singer who heard him in his father's butcher shop crying his father's meats in his beautiful and powerful voice. He later passed into the possession of Harun, who freed him, rewarded him with 100,000 dinars and honored him with a seat by the caliph's side. One evening he went out on the Tigris and started to sing. Immediately torches began to move to and fro in the streets of Baghdad in the hands of people anxious to hear the master singer.

He and other virtuosi of the halcyon days who won undying fame as companions to the caliphs were more than musicians; they were endowed with keen wits and retentive memories well stocked with choice verses of poetry and delightful anecdotes. They were singers, composers, poets and scholars well versed in the scientific lore of the day. Next to them in importance were the instrumentalists among whom the lute was generally most favored; the viol was used by inferior performers. Then came the singing girls,

159

who as a rule performed while concealed behind
curtains. Such singing girls came to be a necessary adornment of the harem and their keeping and training developed into an important
industry. For one of them a messenger of the
governor of Egypt offered 30,000 dinars, which
sum was matched by an envoy of the Byzantine
emperor and increased to 40,000 by a messenger
of the ruler of Khurasan. Her owner capped
the climax by freeing the girl and marrying her.

Among the many Greek works translated in
the golden age of the Abbasids were a few dealing with the speculative theory of music. It was
from these that Arab authors acquired their first
scientific ideas on music and became schooled in
the physical and physiological aspects of the
theory of sound. But on the practical side, they
had purely Arabian models. About this time
the word *musiqi*, later *musiqa* (music), was
borrowed from the Greek and applied to the
theoretical aspects of the science, leaving the
older Arabic term *ghina*, used hitherto for both
song and music, to the practical art. *Qitar*
(guitar) and *urghun* (organ), as names of instruments, and other technical terms of Greek
origin now appear in Arabic. The organ was
clearly an importation from the Byzantines.

Most of the technical treatises unhappily have
been lost in the original. Arabic music, with its
notation and its two constituent elements of
nagham (melodic modes) and *iqa'* (rhythmic
modes), was transmitted by word of mouth only
and has been finally lost. Arabic chants today are

scant in melody but strong in rhythm, and no modern reader can interpret properly the few surviving works on classical music or understand fully the meaning of their ancient designations of rhythm and their scientific terminology.

Cordova: Jewel of the World

While the eastern branch of the Moslem empire was reaching its golden day, the far-western branch in Spain was enjoying a period of corresponding splendor. It was a time of even greater importance to us, for it was chiefly from Moslem Spain that Arab culture advanced to interpenetrate the Christian culture of the early Middle Ages to produce the civilization which we inherited. The climax of this western Moslem civilization came between the ninth and eleventh centuries. But before we can examine it, we must turn back in our story to the year 750.

It was in 750, as we have noted, that the Umayyad dynasty in Damascus was overthrown by the Abbasid family; and, as we have also seen, the accession of the Abbasids to the caliphate was signalized by a ruthless extermination of every

162

member of the defeated house on whom the victors could lay their hands.

Among the very few who escaped was a youth of twenty, Abd-al-Rahman, a striking young man, tall, lean, with sharp, aquiline features and red hair—a youth of exceptional nerve and ability. It was he who made his way to Spain, fought his way to mastery, and kept in power there the Umayyad dynasty which was wiped out in the east.

The story of his escape is dramatic. He was in a Bedouin camp on the left bank of the Euphrates River one day, when horsemen carrying the black standards of the Abbasids suddenly appeared. With his thirteen-year-old brother, Abd-al-Rahman dashed into the river. The younger brother, evidently a poor swimmer, became frightened, heeded the reassurances shouted from the bank that he would be unharmed if he returned, and swam back. He was killed. The older boy kept on and gained the opposite bank.

Afoot, friendless and penniless, he set out southwestward, made his way after great hardships to Palestine, found one friend there and set off again toward the west. In North Africa he barely escaped assassination at the hands of the governor of the province. Wandering from tribe to tribe, always pursued by the spies of the new dynasty, he finally reached Ceuta, five years later. He was a grandson of the tenth caliph of Damascus, and his maternal uncles were Berbers from that district of North Africa. They offered him refuge.

In the south of Spain, across the strait from
Ceuta, were stationed Syrian troops from Damascus. He made his way to them and they accepted him as leader. One southern city after
another opened its gates to him. It took him some
years more to bring all of Spain to subjection,
but he persisted. The Abbasid caliph in Baghdad
appointed a governor of Spain to contest his rule;
two years later that caliph received a gift from
Abd-al-Rahman: the head of his governor, preserved in salt and camphor and wrapped in a
black flag and in the diploma of appointment.
"Thanks be to Allah for having placed the sea
between us and such a foe!" was the caliph's fer-
vent rejoinder. In a passage at arms which has
been immortalized in the literature of the West,
Charlemagne, king of the Franks, also learned
the quality of this redoubtable adversary. Considered an ally of the Abbasid caliph and a
natural enemy of the new amir, or sultan, as
Abd-al-Rahman called himself, Charlemagne
had sent troops in 778 through the northeastern
Spanish marches as far as Saragossa, but had to
withdraw when that city closed its gates in his
face and domestic enemies threatened his authority at home. On its "via dolorosa" of retreat
through the defiles of the Pyrenees, the Frankish
army was attacked in its rear by Basques and
other mountaineers and suffered disastrous losses
in men and baggage. Among the leaders who fell
was Roland. His heroic defense has been immortalized in the *Chanson de Roland*, not only a mas-

terpiece of French literature but one of the most
striking epics of medieval times.

In the process of subduing his adversaries Abd-
al-Rahman developed a well-disciplined, highly
trained army of 40,000 or more mercenary Berbers. He knew how to keep their favor by generous pay. In 757 he discontinued the Friday
sermon hitherto delivered in the name of the Abbasid caliph, but did not assume the caliphal title
himself. He and his successors down to Abd-al-
Rahman III contented themselves with the title
"amir" though ruling independently. Under
Abd-al-Rahman I Spain had thus been the first
province to shake off the authority of the recognized caliph in Islam.

With his realm consolidated and temporarily
pacified, Abd-al-Rahman turned to the arts of
peace, in which he showed himself as great as in
the art of war. He beautified the cities of his
domain, built an aqueduct for the supply of pure
water to the capital, initiated the construction of
a wall round it and erected for himself a palace
and garden outside Cordova in imitation of the
palace built by an ancestor in northeastern Syria.
To his villa he brought water and introduced
exotic plants, such as peaches and pomegranates.
To a lonely palm tree in his garden, said to be the
first imported from Syria, he addressed some
tender and nostalgic verses of his own composition.

Two years before his death in 788 Abd-al-
Rahman founded the great Mosque of Cordova
as a rival to the two sanctuaries of Islam in Jerusa-

lem and Mecca. Completed and enlarged by his successors, it soon became the shrine of Western Islam. With its forest of stately columns and its spacious outer court, this monumental structure, transformed into a Christian cathedral in 1236, has survived to the present day under the popular name "La Mezquita," the mosque. Besides the great mosque the capital could already boast a bridge, over the Guadalquivir (corrupted from an Arabic name meaning "the great river"), later enlarged to seventeen arches. Nor were the interests of the founder of the Umayyad regime limited to the material welfare of his people. In various ways he diligently strove to fashion into one nation Arabians, Syrians, Berbers, Numidians, Hispano-Arabs and Goths—a rather hopeless task; and in more than one sense he initiated the intellectual movement which made Islamic Spain from the ninth to the eleventh centuries one of the two centers of world culture.

Caliph Abd-al-Rahman's court was one of the most glamorous in all Europe. Accredited to it were envoys from the Byzantine emperor as well as from the monarchs of Germany, Italy and France. Its seat, Cordova, with half a million inhabitants, seven hundred mosques and three hundred public baths, yielded in magnificence only to Baghdad and Constantinople. The royal palace, with four hundred rooms and apartments housing thousands of slaves and guards, stood northwest of the town on one of the spurs of the Sierra Morena overlooking the Guadalquivir River. Abd-al-Rahman started its construction

in 936 with money left, so the legend goes, by
one of his concubines who willed that the fund
be used for ransoming captives in Christian
hands; but since none were found he acted on
the suggestion of his other concubine, al-Zahra,
"she with the bright face," and erected this
palatial mansion which he named after her. Marble was brought from Numidia and Carthage;
columns as well as basins with golden statues were
imported or received as presents from Constantinople; and 10,000 workmen with 1,500 beasts
of burden labored on it for a score of years. Enlarged and embellished by later caliphs, al-Zahra
became the nucleus of a royal suburb whose remains, partly excavated in and after 1910, can
still be seen.

In al-Zahra the caliph surrounded himself with
a bodyguard of "Slavs" which numbered 3,750
and headed his standing army of a hundred thousand men. At first applied to slaves and prisoners
captured by Germans and others from among
the Slavonic tribes and sold to the Arabs, the
name Slav was later given to all purchased foreigners: Franks, Galicians, Lombards and the
like, who as a rule were secured young and
Arabicized. With the aid of these "Janissaries" or
"Mamluks" of Spain, the caliph not only kept
treason and brigandage in check but reduced the
influence of the old Arab aristocracy. Commerce
and agriculture flourished and the sources of income for the state were multiplied. The royal
revenue amounted to 6,245,000 dinars, a third
of which sufficed for the army and a third for

167

public works, while the balance was placed in reserve. Never before was Cordova so prosperous, Andalusia so rich and the state so triumphant. All this was achieved through the genius of one man. He died at the ripe age of seventy-three. And he left a statement, we are told, which said that he had known only fourteen days of happiness.

As always, under any dynasty, sovereignty in the Moslem world, West or East, was unstable and precarious. In Spain the Umayyad dynasty kept the nominal rule from the time Abd-al-Rahman I imposed it; but by the time of the ascension of the next outstanding figure in the dynasty, Abd-al-Rahman III, in the year 912, civil disturbances, tribal revolts and general political incompetence on the part of the amirs had reduced the organized Moslem state of Spain to the city of Cordova and its environs.

This third Abd-al-Rahman, like his illustrious predecessor, was a young man when he took office, being only twenty-three; and like him also was a youth of intelligence and determination. One by one he reconquered the lost provinces, reduced them to order and administered them with sagacity and ability. His reign lasted for fifty years, from 912 to 961, an exceptionally long time for that day; it was signalized, politically, by the proclamation by the amir of himself as caliph. With him the Umayyad caliphate in Spain begins. His reign and that of his two immediate successors mark the height of Moslem rule in the West. In this period, roughly the tenth century, the Umayyad capital of Cordova took its place as the most cultured city in Europe and, with Constantinople and Baghdad, as one of the three cultural centers of the world. With its one hundred and thirteen thousand homes, twenty-one suburbs, seventy libraries and numerous bookshops, mosques and palaces, it acquired international fame and inspired awe and admiration in the hearts of travelers. It enjoyed miles of paved streets illuminated by lights from the bordering houses, whereas "seven hundred years after this time there was not so much as one public lamp in London," and "in Paris, centuries subsequently, whoever stepped over his threshold on a rainy day stepped up to his ankles in mud."

The Arab attitude toward the Nordic barbarians found expression in the words of the learned Toledan judge Said, who thought that "because the sun does not shed its rays directly over their heads, their climate is cold and atmosphere clouded. Consequently their temperaments have become cold and their humors rude, while their bodies have grown large, their complexion light and their hair long. They lack withal sharpness of wit and penetration of intellect, while stupidity and folly prevail among them." Whenever the rulers of Leon, Navarre or Barcelona needed a surgeon, an architect, a master singer, or a dressmaker, it was to Cordova that they applied. The fame of the Moslem capital penetrated distant Germany, where a Saxon nun styled it "the jewel of the world."

Spain under the caliphate was one of the wealthiest and most thickly populated lands of Europe. The capital boasted some thirteen thousand weavers and a flourishing leather industry. From Spain the art of tanning and embossing leather was carried to Morocco and from these two lands it was brought to France and England, as the terms cordovan, cordwainer and morocco indicate. Wool and silk were woven not only in Cordova but in Malaga, Almeria and other centers. The raising of silkworms, originally a monopoly of the Chinese, was introduced by Moslems into Spain, where it thrived. Almeria also produced glassware and brasswork. Paterna in Valencia was the home of pottery. Jaen and Algarve were noted for their mines of gold and silver, Cordova for its iron and lead and Malaga for its rubies. Toledo, like Damascus, was famous all over the world for its swords. The art of inlaying steel and other metals with gold and silver and decorating them with flower patterns, an art introduced from Damascus, flourished in several Spanish and other European centers and left a linguistic heritage in such words as damascene and damaskeen.

The Spanish Arabs introduced agricultural methods practiced in Western Asia. They dug canals, cultivated grapes and introduced, among other plants and fruits, rice, apricots, peaches, pomegranates, oranges, sugar cane, cotton and saffron. The southeastern plains of the peninsula, especially favored by climate and soil, developed important centers of rural and urban activity. Here wheat and other grains, as well as olives and sundry fruits, were raised by a peasantry who worked the soil on shares with the owners.

This agricultural development was one of the glories of Moslem Spain and one of the Arabs' lasting gifts to the land, for Spanish gardens have preserved to this day a "Moorish" character. One of the best-known gardens is the Generalife—a word which comes from the Arabic *jannat al-'arif*, "the inspector's paradise"—a monument of the late thirteenth century whose villa was one of the outlying buildings of the Alhambra. This garden, "proverbial for its extensive shades, falling waters and soft breeze," was terraced in the form of an amphitheater and irrigated by streams which, after forming numerous cascades, lost themselves among the flowers, shrubs and trees represented today by a few gigantic cypresses and myrtles.

The industrial and agricultural products of Moslem Spain were more than sufficient for domestic consumption. Seville, one of the greatest of its river ports, exported cotton, olives and oil; it imported cloth and slaves from Egypt and singing girls from Europe and Asia. The exports of Malaga and Jaen included saffron, figs, marble and sugar. Through Alexandria and Constantinople Spanish products found markets as far away as India and Central Asia. Especially active was the trade with Damascus, Baghdad and Mecca. The international nautical vocabulary of the modern world contains not a few words

which testify to the former Arab supremacy on
the seas—admiral, arsenal, average, cable, shal-
lop.

The government maintained a regular postal
service. It modeled its coinage on Eastern patterns, with the dinar as the gold unit and the dir-
ham as the silver unit. Arab money was in use
in the Christian kingdoms of the north, which
for nearly four hundred years had no coinage
other than Arabic or French.

The real glory of this period, however, lies in
fields other than political. Al-Hakam, Abd-al-
Rahman's successor, was himself a scholar and
patronized learning. He granted munificent
bounties to scholars and established twenty-seven
free schools in the capital. Under him the University of Cordova, founded in the principal
mosque by Abd-al-Rahman III, rose to a place
of preeminence among the educational institutions of the world. It preceded both al-Azhar of
Cairo and the Nizamiyah of Baghdad, and attracted students, Christian and Moslem, not only
from Spain but from other parts of Europe,
Africa and Asia. Al-Hakam enlarged the mosque
which housed the university, conducted water
to it in lead pipes and decorated it with mosaics
brought by Byzantine artists. He invited professors from the East to the university and set aside
endowments for their salaries.

In addition to the university the capital
housed a library of first magnitude. Al-Hakam
was a bibliophile; his agents ransacked the bookshops of Alexandria, Damascus and Baghdad

with a view to buying or copying manuscripts. The books thus gathered are said to have numbered 400,000, their titles filling a catalogue of forty-four volumes, in each one of which twenty sheets were devoted to poetical works alone. Al-Hakam, probably the best scholar among Moslem caliphs, personally used several of these works; his marginal notes on certain manuscripts rendered them highly prized by later collectors. In order to secure the first copy of the *Aghani*, which al-Isbahani, a descendant of the Umayyads, was then composing in Iraq, al-Hakam sent the author a thousand dinars. The general state of culture in Andalusia reached such a high level at this time that the distinguished Dutch scholar Dozy went so far as to declare enthusiastically that "nearly everyone could read and write"— all this when in Christian Europe only the rudiments of learning were known and that chiefly by a few churchmen.

Contributions to the West

A favorite inscription over collegiate portals in Moslem Spain reads: "The world is supported by four things only: the learning of the wise, the justice of the great, the prayers of the righteous and the valor of the brave."

It is significant that in this European statement of Moslem ideals, learning comes first. The strength of Arab arms impressed itself deeply on the Western world, but the impression was not lasting; the Arab faith never appealed strongly to the European imagination; the Arab idea of justice set few precedents; but Moslem learning entered Western thought at many a point. Moslem Spain wrote one of the brightest chapters in the intellectual history of medieval Europe. Between the middle of the eighth and the beginning of the thirteenth centuries, as we have noted before, the Arabic-speaking peoples were the main bearers of the torch of culture and civilization throughout the world, the medium through which ancient science and philosophy were recovered, supplemented and transmitted to make possible the renaissance of Western Europe. The greatest scholar and the most original thinker of Spanish Islam was Ali ibn-Hazm, who lived from 994 to 1064, one of the two or three most fertile minds and most prolific writers of Islam. Biographers ascribe to him four hundred volumes on history, theology, tradition, logic, poetry and allied subjects. The most valuable of his surviving work is one which entitles him to the honor of being the first scholar in the field of comparative religion. In this work he pointed out difficulties in the biblical narratives which disturbed no other minds till the rise of the higher criticism in the sixteenth century.

In prose, the fables, tales and apologues which began to flourish in Western Europe during the thirteenth century present unmistakable analogies with earlier Arabic works, themselves of Indo-Persian origin. The delightful fables of *Kalilah wa-Dimnah* were translated into Spanish for Alfonso the Wise (1252-1284) of Castile and Leon, and shortly afterward into Latin by a baptized Jew. A Persian translation became through French one of the sources of La Fontaine, as acknowledged by the poet himself. To the *maqamah*, written in rhymed prose adorned with all manner of philological curiosity and intended to teach some moral lesson through the adven-

5

5

tures of a cavalier-hero, the Spanish picaresque novel bears close affinity. But the most significant contribution of Arabic to the literature of medieval Europe was the influence it exercised by its form, which helped liberate Western imagination from a narrow and rigid discipline circumscribed by convention. The rich fantasy of Spanish literature betrays Arabic models, as does the wit of Cervantes' *Don Quixote*, whose author was once a prisoner in Algiers and jokingly claimed that the book had an original in Arabic.

Wherever and whenever the Arabic language was used, the passion for poetical composition was intense. Verses countless in number passed from mouth to mouth and were admired by high and low. This sheer joy in the beauty and euphony of words, a characteristic of Arabic-speaking peoples, manifested itself on Spanish soil. The first Umayyad sovereign was a poet and so were several of his successors. Most of the sovereigns had poets-laureate attached to their courts and took them along on their travels and wars. Seville boasted the largest number of grateful and inspired poets, but the flame had been kindled long before in Cordova and later shone brilliantly at Granada as long as that city remained the bulwark of Islam.

Ibn-Zaydun (1003-1071), an important and characteristic poet, belonged to a noble Arab family, and was first a confidential agent to the chief of the Cordovan oligarchy. He later fell from grace, probably on account of his violent love for the poetess Walladah, daughter of a caliph, but after several years in prison and exile was appointed to the twofold position of grand vizir and commander of the troops and given the title "he of the two vizirates," that of the sword and that of the pen. This beautiful and talented Walladah, who died in 1087, renowned alike for personal charm and literary ability, was the Sappho of Spain. Arab women in Spain seem to have shown special taste and aptitude for poetry and literature.

Emancipated to a limited degree from the fetters of convention, Spanish Arabic poetry developed new metrical forms and acquired an almost modern sensibility to the beautiful in nature. Through its ballads and love songs it manifested a romantic feeling which anticipated the attitude of medieval chivalry. Music and song established and maintained everywhere their alliance with poetry.

It was Arabic poetry in general and the lyric type in particular that aroused native Christian admiration and became one of the potent factors in assimilation. Two of the lyric forms developed into the Castilian popular verse form of *villancico*, which was extensively used for Christian hymns, including Christmas carols.

The emergence of a definite literary scheme of Platonic love in Spanish as early as the eighth century marks a distinctive contribution of Arabic poetry. In southern France the first Provençal poets appear full-fledged toward the end of the eleventh century with palpitating love expressed in a wealth of fantastic imagery. The troubadours

177

who flourished in the twelfth century imitated their southern contemporaries, the *zajal*-singers. Following the Arabic precedent, the Cult of the Dame suddenly arises in southwestern Europe. The *Chanson de Roland*, the noblest monument of early European literature, whose appearance prior to 1080 marks the beginning of a new civilization—that of Western Europe—owes its existence to a military contact with Moslem Spain, just as the Homeric poems mark the beginning of historic Greece.

Primary education, widely diffused as we have seen, was based, as in all Moslem lands, on writing and reading from the Koran and on Arabic grammar and poetry. The position of women in the learned life proves that in Andalusia the maxims prohibiting the teaching of writing to women were but little applied. Higher education was based on koranic exegesis and theology, philosophy, Arabic grammar, poetry and lexicography, history and geography. Several of the principal towns possessed what might be called universities, chief among which were those of Cordova, Seville, Malaga and Granada. The University of Cordova included among its departments astronomy, mathematics and medicine, in addition to theology and law. Its enrollment must have reached into thousands and its certificate opened the way to the most lucrative posts in the realm. At the University of Granada the curriculum comprised theology, jurisprudence, medicine, chemistry, philosophy and astronomy. Castilian and other foreign students patronized this institution.

Side by side with the universities, libraries flourished. The royal library of Cordova became the largest and best. A number of persons, including some women, had private collections. The peculiarities of Moslem life with its lack of political assemblies and theaters, which were characteristic features of Greece and Rome, made books almost the sole means of acquiring knowledge.

This accumulation of books in Andalusia would not have been possible but for the local manufacture of writing paper, one of the most beneficial contributions of Islam to Europe, as we have noticed in our study of Baghdad. From Morocco, into which the manufacture of paper was introduced from the East, the industry passed into Spain in the middle of the twelfth century. A philological reminder of this historical fact is English "ream," which is derived through Old French *rayme* from Spanish *resma*, a loan word from Arabic *rizmah*, a bundle. After Spain the art of papermaking was established in Italy, about 1270, also as a result of Moslem influence, presumably from Sicily. France owed its first paper mills to Spain, and not to returning Crusaders as claimed by some. From these countries the industry spread throughout Europe. A secretary of Abd-al-Rahman used to write the official communications in his home and send them to a special office for reproduction

179

—a form of printing (*tab'*, lithography)—
whence copies were distributed to the various
governmental agents.

After the destruction of Moslem power in
Spain less than two thousand volumes survived
to be collected by Philip II (1556-1598) and
his successors from the various Arab libraries.
These formed the nucleus of the Escurial library
still standing not far from Madrid. An interesting
tale explains how other volumes were added.
Early in the seventeenth century the sultan of Morocco, fleeing his capital, sent his library abroad
a ship whose captain refused to land the books at
the proper destination because he had not received full pay in advance. On its way to
Marseille the ship fell into the hands of Spanish
pirates and its bookish booty, to the number of
three or four thousand volumes, was deposited
by order of Philip III in the Escurial, which
made this library one of the richest in Arabic
manuscripts.

The two names which stand for the highest
literary accomplishment and historical compre-
hension of which Western Islam was capable are
those of the two friends, ibn-al-Khatib and ibn-
Khaldun. In 1371 ibn-al-Khatib, who was a vizir,
fled from Granada because of court intrigues,
only to be strangled to death three years later at
Fas as a result of a private feud. In his death Granada, if not the whole of Arab Spain, lost its last
important author, poet and statesman. Of the
sixty odd works penned by ibn-al-Khatib—poetical, historical, geographical, medical and phil-

osophical—about a third have survived. Of
these the most important for us is the extensive
history of Granada.

The fame of ibn-Khaldun rests on his *Mu-
qaddamah*, an introduction to history. In it he
presented for the first time a theory of historical
development which takes due cognizance of the
physical facts of climate and geography as well
as of moral and spiritual forces. As one who endeavored to find and formulate laws of national
progress and decay, ibn-Khaldun may be considered the discoverer—as he himself claimed—
of the true scope and nature of history or at least
the real founder of social science. No Arab
writer, indeed no European, had ever before
taken a view of history at once so comprehensive
and philosophic. By the consensus of all critical
opinion ibn-Khaldun, who died in 1406, was the
greatest historical philosopher Islam produced
and one of the greatest of all time.

Arab geographical studies had but a limited
influence in the West, but they kept alive the
ancient doctrine that the earth was round. We
have already referred to the Hindu idea that
the known hemisphere of the world had a center
or "world cupola" situated at an equal distance
from the four cardinal points. This *arin* theory
found its way into a Latin work published in
1410 and from this Columbus acquired the doctrine which made him believe that the earth was
shaped in the form of a pear and that on the western hemisphere opposite the *arin* was a corresponding elevated center.

In the realm of astronomical geography and mathematics a number of new concepts were contributed to Western lore. In Spain astronomical studies were cultivated assiduously after the middle of the tenth century and were regarded with special favor by the rulers of Cordova, Seville and Toledo. Most of the Andalusian astronomers believed in astral influence as the cause of most events between birth and death on this earth. The study of this astral influence, i.e. astrology, necessitated the determining of the location of places throughout the world together with their latitudes and longitudes. Thus astrology became the mother of astronomy. It was through Spanish channels that the Latin West found its Oriental inspiration in astronomy and astrology. The leading Moslem astronomical works were translated in Spain into Latin, and the Alfonsine tables compiled by Alfonso X in the thirteenth century were nothing but a development of Arab astronomy. From their studies of the stars, Arab authors gave us also the first chapters on spherical and plane trigonometry—for, like algebra and analytical geometry, the science of trigonometry was largely founded by Arabs. Everyone who reads the names of stars on an ordinary celestial sphere can readily discern that Arab astronomers have left on the sky immortal traces of their industry. Not only are most of the star names in European languages of Arabic origin, such as Acrab (*aqrab*, scorpion), Algedi (*al-jadi*, the kid), Altair (*al-ta'-ir*, the flyer), Deneb (*dhanab*, tail), Pherkad (*farqad*, calf), but a number of technical terms, including "azimuth" (*al-sumut*), "nadir" (*nazir*), "zenith" (*al-samt*), are likewise of Arabic etymology and testify to the rich legacy of Islam to Christian Europe.

One of the most interesting mathematical terms borrowed from Arabic is "cipher" or "zero." While the Arabs did not invent the cipher, they nevertheless introduced it with the Arabic numerals into Europe and taught Westerners the employment of this most convenient convention, thus facilitating the use of arithmetic in everyday life. Without the zero we should have to arrange our figures in a table with columns of units, tens, hundreds, etc.; that is, use an abacus.

Diffusion of the Arabic numerals in non-Moslem Europe was incredibly slow. Christian arithmeticians throughout the eleventh, twelfth and part of the thirteenth centuries persisted in the use of the antiquated Roman numerals and the abacus, or made a compromise and used the new algorisms together with their old system. It was in Italy that the new symbols were first employed for practical purposes. In 1202 Leonardo Fibonacci of Pisa, who was taught by a Moslem master and had traveled in North Africa, published a work which was the main landmark in the introduction of the Arabic numerals. More than that, it marks the beginning of European mathematics. With the old type of numerals, arithmetical progress along certain lines would have been impossible. The zero and

183

Arabic numerals lie behind the science of calculation as we know it today.

In the field of natural history, especially botany pure and applied, as in that of astronomy and mathematics, the Western Moslems enriched the world by their researches. They made correct observations on sexual difference between such plants as palms and hemps and classified plants into those that grow from cuttings, those that grow from seed and those that they thought grow spontaneously. A treatise on agriculture by ibn-al-Awwam of Seville—toward the end of the twelfth century—is not only the most important Islamic, but the outstanding medieval, work on the subject. Derived partly from earlier Greek and Arabic sources and partly from the experience of Moslem husbandmen in Spain, this book treats of five hundred and eighty-five plants and explains the cultivation of more than fifty fruit trees. It presents new observations on grafting and the properties of soil and manure and discusses the symptoms of several diseases of trees and vines, suggesting methods of cure.

The best-known botanist and pharmacist of Spain, in fact of the Moslem world, was ibn-al-Baytar, who died in Damascus in 1248, leaving the foremost medieval treatise on "simple remedies."

Most of the Spanish Arab physicians were physicians by avocation and something else by vocation. Ibn-al-Khatib, whom we have already noted as a stylist and historian, held like many other physicians a vizirial office. In connection

with the "black death," which in the middle of
the fourteenth century was ravaging Europe and
before which Christians stood helpless, considering it an act of God, this Moslem physician of
Granada composed a treatise in defense of the
theory of infection, which has a genuinely scientific ring:

"To those who say, 'How can we admit the
possibility of infection while the religious law
denies it?' we reply that the existence of contagion is established by experience, investigation,
the evidence of the senses and trustworthy reports. These facts constitute a sound argument.
The fact of infection becomes clear to the in-
vestigator who notices how he who establishes
contact with the afflicted gets the disease, whereas he who is not in contact remains safe, and how
transmission is effected through garments, vessels
and earrings."

In the first centuries of Moslem domination
in Spain, Eastern culture flowed from a higher
level into Andalusia. Spanish savants journeyed
"in quest of learning" to Egypt, Syria,
Iraq, Persia and even Transoxiana and China; but
in the eleventh and following centuries the
course was reversed and the current became
strong enough in the twelfth century to overflow into Europe. In the transmission of Arab
medicine to Europe, northwestern Africa and
Spain—in particular Toledo, where Gerard of
Cremona and Michael Scot worked—played
the leading part. Thereby were the three main
medical traditions, Moslem, Jewish and Chris-

tian, at last brought into a position where they could be amalgamated. Through these and similar translations several Arabic technical terms were introduced into European languages. "Julep" (Arabic *julab*, from Persian *gulab*, rose water), for a medicinal aromatic drink, and "syrup" (Arabic *sharab*), a solution of sugar in water made according to an officinal formula and often medicated with some special therapeutic, may serve as illustrations. "Soda," which in medieval Latin meant headache and in the form *sodanum* headache remedy, comes ultimately from Arabic *suda'*, splitting pain in the head. Among chemical terms which passed into European languages through Latin from Arabic works we may note "alcohol," "alembic," "alkali," and "antimony."

The crowning achievement of the intellectual class of Arabs in Spain was in the realm of philosophic thought. Here they formed the last and strongest link in the chain which transmitted Greek philosophy, as transmuted by them and their Eastern coreligionists, to the Latin West, adding their own contribution, especially in reconciling faith and reason, religion and science. To the Moslem thinkers Aristotle was truth, Plato was truth, the Koran was truth; but truth must be one. Hence arose the necessity of harmonizing the three, and to this task they addressed themselves. The Christian scholastics were faced by the same problem, but their task was rendered more difficult by the accumulation of dogmas and mysteries in their theology. Philosophy as developed by the Greeks and monotheistic religion as evolved by the Hebrew prophets were, as we have noted before, the richest legacies of the ancient West and of the ancient East.

This first influx into Western Europe of a body of new ideas, mainly philosophic and medical, marks the beginning of the end of the "Dark Ages" and the dawn of the scholastic period. Kindled by contact with Arab thought and quickened by fresh acquaintance with ancient Greek lore, the interest of Europeans in scholarship and philosophy led them rapidly on to an independent intellectual life of their own, whose fruits we still enjoy.

We can mention here only a few of the many great philosophers of Islamic Spain. Ibn-Tufayl, who died in 1185, was among the outstanding. His masterpiece was an original philosophic romance entitled *Hayy ibn-Yaqzan*, "the living one, son of the vigilant," whose underlying idea was that human capacity unassisted by external agency may attain to the knowledge of the higher world and may find out by degrees its dependence upon a Supreme Being. This story, one of the most delightful and original in the literature of the Middle Ages, was first translated into Latin by Edward Pococke, the Younger, in 1671 and then into most European languages, including Dutch in 1672, Russian in 1920 and Spanish as recently as 1934. Some have sought in it an original of *Robinson Crusoe*.

The greatest Moslem philosopher, judged by

187

his influence especially over the West, was the Hispano-Arab astronomer, physician and Aristotelian commentator Averroës (in Arabic ibn-Rushd), who was born in Cordova in 1126. Averroës' chief contribution to medicine was a work in which the fact is recognized that no one is taken twice by smallpox and the function of the retina is accurately described. In the Jewish and Christian world, however, he was known primarily as a commentator on Aristotle. A medieval commentator, we should recall, was an author who composed a scientific or philosophic work using some earlier writing as a background and framework. Accordingly, Averroës' commentaries were a series of treatises using in part the titles of Aristotle's works and paraphrasing their contents. He belonged more to Christian Europe than to Moslem Asia or Africa. To the West he became "the commentator" as Aristotle was "the teacher." The minds of the Christian schoolmen and scholars of medieval Europe were agitated by Averroës' Aristotle as by no other author. From the end of the twelfth to the end of the sixteenth century Averroism remained the dominant school of thought, and that in spite of the orthodox religious reaction it created first among the Moslems in Spain, then among the Talmudists and finally among the Christian clergy. Averroës was a rationalist and claimed the right to submit everything save the revealed dogmas of faith to the judgment of reason; but he was not, as believed by many, the father of free thought and unbelief and the great enemy of faith. Earlier Moslem Aristotelians had taken for genuine a number of apocryphal works, including some of Neo-Platonic character; Averroës' philosophy involved a return to purer and more scientific Aristotelianism. After being purged of objectionable matter by ecclesiastical authorities, his writings became prescribed studies in the University of Paris and other institutions of higher learning. With all its excellences and all the misconceptions collected under its name, the intellectual movement initiated by Averroës continued to be a living factor in European thought until the birth of modern experimental science.

For first place after Averroës among the philosophers of the age the only candidate is his Jewish contemporary and fellow Cordovan ibn-Maymun, the renowned Mosheh Maimon, or Maimonides, the most famous of the Hebrew physicians and philosophers of the whole Arabic epoch. He was born in Cordova in 1135, but his family left the country as a result of Moslem persecution and settled in Cairo about 1165. The claim of certain biographers that in Spain he professed Islam in public but practiced Judaism in secret has recently been subjected to sharp criticism. In Cairo he became the court physician of the celebrated Saladin and of his son. From 1177 on he held the chief religious office of the Jewish community at Cairo, where he died in 1204. In accordance with his will his body was carried by hand over the route once taken by Moses and buried in Tiberias, where his unpretentious tomb is still visited by throngs of pilgrims. Ailing people among the poor Jews of modern Egypt still seek their cure by spending the night in the underground chamber of the Synagogue of Rabbi Mosheh ben-Maimon in Cairo. A popular Jewish saying, "From Moses to Moses there was none like Moses [Maimonides]," expresses the eminent position he has ever held in Jewish estimation.

Maimonides distinguished himself as astronomer, theologian, physician and above all as philosopher. He improved the method of circumcision, ascribed hemorrhoids to constipation, prescribing for them a light diet predominantly vegetarian, and held advanced ideas on hygiene. His leading philosophical work bore the title *Dalalat al-Ha'irin*, the guide of the perplexed, and in this he tried to reconcile Jewish theology with Moslem Aristotelianism or, in broader terms, faith with reason. Prophetic visions he explained as psychical experiences. To this extent at least he stood as the champion of scientific thought against biblical "fundamentalism" and aroused the anger of conservative theologians, who referred to his book as *Dalalah*, misguidance. His philosophic ideas as expressed in this and other works resembled those of Averroës, though developed independently. Like Averroës he knew no Greek and depended entirely on Arabic translations. The theory of creation which he propounded, but did not share, was the atomistic one as distinguished from the two others held by the Arabic-writing thinkers;

namely, the fundamentalist theory, which made God creator of everything, and the philosophical, which was Neo-Platonic and Aristotelian. His works, with one exception, were all written in Arabic, but in Hebrew characters, and were soon translated into Hebrew and later in part into Latin. Their influence, far-reaching in space and time, was exerted mainly over Jews and Christians. Down to the eighteenth century they remained the principal medium through which Jewish thought reached the Gentiles. Modern critics detect traces of that influence in the Dominicans, as attested by the works of Albertus Magnus, in Albertus' rival, Duns Scotus, in Spinoza and even in Kant.

The ruling mystic of the age was another Hispano-Arab, ibn-Arabi, the greatest speculative genius of Islamic Sufism. Ibn-Arabi flourished in Seville but died in Damascus in 1240, where his tomb is still standing. In one of his works he develops the theme of the nocturnal journey of Muhammad and his ascension to Heaven in which he anticipates the masterpiec of Dante.

By the close of the thirteenth century Arabic science and philosophy had been transmitted to Europe. The intellectual avenue leading from the portals of Toledo through the Pyrenees wound its way through Provence and the Alpine passes into Lorraine, Germany and Central Europe and across the Channel into England. Marseille, Toulouse, Narbonne, Montpellier were French centers of Arabic thought. In eastern

France Cluny, whose famous abbey housed a number of Spanish monks, was during the twelfth century a significant focus for the diffusion of Arab learning. Its abbot, Peter the Venerable, sponsored in 1141 the first Latin translation of the Koran, besides various pamphlets directed against Islam. Arabic science, introduced into Lorraine or Lotharingia in the tenth century made that region a center of scientific influence in the following two centuries. Liège, Gorze and Cologne, among other Lotharingian cities, provided the most fertile soil for the germination of Arab learning. From Lorraine it radiated into other parts of Germany and was transported into Norman England by men born or educated in Lorraine. Spanish Arabic learning had permeated all Western Europe. Spain's work as an intermediary was done.

The Cross Supplants the Crescent

If anything parallels the astounding rapidity with which the sons of the Arabian desert conquered most of the civilized world in the first Islamic century, it is the swift decadence of Arab domination between the middle of the third and the middle of the fourth centuries after the death of Muhammad. About A.D. 820 more extensive authority was concentrated in the hands of one man, the caliph in Baghdad, than in those of any other living person; by 920 the power of his successor had so diminished that it was hardly felt even in his capital city. By 1258 that city itself lay in ruins. With its fall Arab hegemony was lost forever and the history of the real caliphate closed.

Among the external factors the barbarian (in this case Mongol or Tartar) onslaughts, though spectacular in themselves, were in reality only contributory to the final downfall. Even the rise, mushroom-like, of the numberless dynasties and quasi-dynasties in the heart of the caliphate and on its periphery was in itself a symptom of the disease rather than the cause of it. As in the case of the Roman Empire of the West, the sick man was already on his deathbed when the burglars burst open the doors and snatched their share of the imperial heritage.

The caliphate was going to pieces. Many of the original conquests were only nominal to begin with, and the method of administration was not conducive to stability and continuity. Exploitation and overtaxation were recognized policies, not the exception but the rule. Lines of cleavage between Arabs and non-Arabs, between Arab Moslems and Neo-Moslems, between Moslems and dhimmis, remained sharply marked. Among the Arabians themselves the old divisive feeling between north and south persisted. Neither the Iranian Persians, nor the Turanian Turks, nor the Hamitic Berbers were ever welded into a homogeneous whole with the Semitic Arabians. No consciousness of kind knit these diverse elements closely together. The sons of Iran were ever mindful of their ancient national glory and never reconciled themselves entirely to the new regime. The Berbers vaguely expressed their tribal feeling and sense of difference by their readiness to embrace any schismatic movement. The people of Syria long expected the rise of a leader to deliver them from the Abbasid yoke. Within the fold of religion itself centrifugal forces, no less potent than the political and military, were active, producing Shiites, Qarmatians, Ismailites, Assassins and the like. Several of these groupings represented more than religious sects; the Qarmatians staggered the eastern part of the empire with their blows, and soon afterward the Fatimids seized the west. Islam was no more able to unite its devotees into a corporate whole than was the caliphate to incorporate the lands of the Mediterranean with those of Central Asia into a stable unit.

Then there were the social and moral forces of disintegration. The blood of the conquering element became in the course of centuries diluted with that of the conquered, with a subsequent loss of their dominating position and qualities. With the decay of the Arab national life, Arab stamina and morale broke down. Gradually the empire developed into an empire of the conquered. The harem, made possible by the countless number of eunuchs; the girl and the boy slaves, *ghilman,* who contributed most to the degradation of womanhood and the degeneration of manhood; the unlimited concubines and the numberless half brothers and half sisters in the imperial household with their unavoidable jealousies and intrigues; luxurious living with its emphasis on wine and song—all these and similar forces sapped the vitality of family life. The position of the already feeble heirs to the throne was rendered still more uncertain by their interminable disputes over the right of succession.

Economic factors were likewise important. The imposition of taxes and the government of the provinces for the benefit of the ruling class discouraged farming and industry. As the rulers grew rich the people grew proportionately poor. Within the states grew smaller states whose lords habitually robbed their serfs. The depletion of manpower by the recurring bloody strife left many a cultivated farm desolate. Floods in lower Mesopotamia periodically wrought havoc, and famines in various parts of the empire added their quota of disaster. The frequent spread of epidemics—plague, smallpox, malaria and other fevers—before which medieval man stood powerless, decimated the population in large areas. No less than forty major epidemics are recorded in the Arabic annals of the first four centuries after the conquest.

The causes of the disintegration of Moslem power in Spain and other parts of Europe were on the whole of the same nature as those which brought about the collapse of the caliphate in the eastern and central parts of the empire, save that the death blow here was delivered by Christian rather than Mongol arms.

From the ruins of the Umayyad caliphate of Cordova, which fell in 1031, there emerged a conglomeration of petty Moslem states which spent themselves in fratricidal quarrels. No less than twenty such short-lived states arose in as many towns or provinces. The primacy among them lay first with Seville, whose court enjoyed a period of glory second to that of Cordova. Before the century was over, Seville, among other states, fell a prey to a newly rising power, a Berber dynasty from Morocco. The period of Berber hegemony in Spain had begun.

This Berber dynasty which controlled both northwestern Africa and Spain was called Almoravides. The name is a corruption of an Arabic word which means "warrior monks." Originally a military brotherhood, the Almoravides drew their first recruits from tribes whose men wore veils covering the face below the eyes, as their descendants the Touareg still do to the present day. Hence the other name they acquired, the "Veil Wearers." Another Berber dynasty followed the Almoravides. Among the Arab dynasties worthy of note was the Nasrid of Granada, one of whose members, Muhammad al-Ghalib, who ruled from 1232 to 1273, built the world-renowned Alhambra.

We are not concerned in tracing the vicissitudes of the petty dynasties, east or west, which marked the process of disintegration. But the main outline of that story is worth noting, especially in the story of the later days of Moslem power in Europe, the interesting and always significant evidence of the tendency of contrasting men and cultures to blend and harmonize, even at the times when they were most ferociously bent upon exterminating one another. In man's

197

power to pass on his learning and his art lies the clue to most of that which is noble and enduring in his civilization.

The period of Christian reconquest in Spain started as early as the fall of the Umayyad caliphate in the eleventh century. In fact, Spanish historians consider the battle of Covadonga in 718, in which the Asturian chieftain Pelayo checked Moslem advance, as marking the actual beginning of reconquest. Had the Moslems in the eighth century destroyed the last vestiges of Christian power in the mountainous north, the subsequent story of Spain might have been entirely different. Impeded at first by constant friction among the Christian chiefs of the north, the process of reclamation was greatly accelerated by the final union of Castile and Leon in 1230. By the middle of the thirteenth century the reconquest was practically completed, with the exception of Granada. Toledo fell in 1085; Cordova followed in 1236 and Seville in 1248.

After the middle of the thirteenth century two major processes were in operation; the Christianizing of Spain and its unification. Christianizing the country was different from reconquering and unifying it. The only part of the peninsula where Islam had struck root was where the earlier Semitic, Carthaginian, civilization had once flourished. The same was true of Sicily, a fact not without significance. In general the line of cleavage between Islam and Christianity coincided with the ancient line between the Punic and Occidental civilizations. By the thirteenth century many Moslems throughout the land had become subject to the Christians either by conquest or treaty, but had otherwise preserved their laws and religion. Such Moslems were designated Mudejars, from an Arabic word meaning "domesticated." Many of the Mudejars were now forgetting their Arabic, adopting exclusively the Romance tongue and becoming more or less assimilated to the Christians.

Progress toward the final unification of Spain was slow but sure. At this time the Christian territory was made up of but two kingdoms, Castile and Aragon. The marriage in 1469 of Ferdinand of Aragon to Isabella of Castile united permanently the crowns of these two kingdoms. This union spelled doom for Moslem power in Spain. The late Nasrid sultans were by no means able to cope with the increasing danger. The last of them were involved in dynastic troubles which rendered their position still more precarious. Of the twenty-one sultans who ruled from 1232 to 1492, six ruled twice and one ruled three times. On January 2, 1492, a date that impinges on the beginning of the history of America, Christian troops entered Granada after a long and fierce siege. "The Cross supplanted the Crescent."

Their Catholic Majesties Ferdinand and Isabella failed to abide by the terms of the capitulation. Under the leadership of the Queen's confessor, Cardinal Ximenez de Cisneros, a campaign of forced conversion was inaugurated in 1499. The cardinal at first tried to eliminate Arabic books dealing with Islam by burning them.

Granada was the scene of a bonfire of Arabic manuscripts. The Inquisition was then instituted and kept busy. All Moslems who remained in the country after the capture of Granada were now called Moriscos, Spanish for "little Moors." The Romans called Western Africa Mauretania and its inhabitants Mauri (presumably of Phoenician origin meaning "western"), whence the Spanish *Moro*, and the English Moor. The Berbers were the Moors proper, but the term was conventionally applied to all Moslems of Spain and northwestern Africa. The half million Moslems of the Philippines are still known by the name of Moros, given them by the Spaniards on the discovery of the islands by Magellan in 1521. The term Morisco was applied originally to Spaniards converted into Islam.

The Moslem Spaniards spoke a Romance dialect but employed the Arabic script. Many, if not most, Moriscos were of course of Spanish descent, but all were now "reminded" that their ancestors had been Christians and that they must either submit to baptism or suffer the consequences. The Mudejars were grouped with the Moriscos and many became crypto-Moslems, professing Christianity but secretly practicing Islam. Some would come home from their Christian weddings to be married secretly by the Moslem rite; many would adopt a Christian name for public and an Arabic one for private use. As early as 1501 a royal decree was issued declaring that all Moslems in Castile and Leon should either recant or leave Spain, but evidently it was not strictly applied. In 1526 the Moslems of Aragon were confronted with the same alternatives. In 1556 Philip II promulgated a law requiring the remaining Moslems to abandon at once their language, worship, institutions and manner of life. He even ordered the destruction of the Spanish baths as a relic of infidelity. A rising, the second of its kind, started in Granada and spread to the neighboring mountains, but was put down. The final order of expulsion was signed by Philip III in 1609, resulting in the forcible deportation en masse of practically all Moslems on Spanish soil. Some half a million are said to have suffered this fate, having been forced to embark for the shores of Africa or to take ship to more distant lands of Islam. It was mainly from these Moriscos that the ranks of the Moroccan corsairs were recruited. Between the fall of Granada and the first decade of the seventeenth century it is estimated that about three million Moslems were banished or executed. The Moorish problem was forever solved for Spain, which thus became the conspicuous exception to the rule that wherever Arab civilization was planted there it was permanently fixed. "The Moors were banished; for a while Christian Spain shone, like the moon, with a borrowed light; then came the eclipse, and in that darkness Spain has grovelled ever since."

All monuments of religious art in Spain have perished with the exception of one of the earliest and grandest, the great Mosque of Cordova. The foundation was laid in 786 on the site of a Christian church which was originally a Roman temple. The main part of the mosque, with the square minaret, was completed in 793. The Spanish minarets followed the African style, which was of Syrian origin. Twelve hundred and ninety-three columns, a veritable forest, supported its roof. Brass lanterns made from Christian bells illuminated the building. "One chandelier held a thousand lights; the smallest held twelve." For the decoration of the building Byzantine craftsmen were employed, as they may have been employed in the Umayyad mosques of Syria. Eighty thousand gold pieces from the spoils of the Goths were spent on the structure by its founder. Enlargements and repairs were made on it by Moslems down to the year 1000. Today it is a cathedral to the Virgin of the Assumption.

Of the secular monuments the Alcazar (an Arabic word) of Seville and the Alhambra of Granada, with their profuse but graceful decorations, are the most superb remains. The oldest part of the Alcazar of Seville was built by a Toledan architect for an Almohade governor in 1199-1200. The Almohades were the second Berber dynasty, after the Almoravides, to rule over Moslem Spain and acquired their name from an Arabic word meaning "unitarians." The Alcazar was restored in the Moslem style by Mudejar workmen for King Peter the Cruel in 1353, and was used until a few years ago as a royal residence. Among the many Alcazars in Cordova, Toledo and other Spanish towns, this of

Seville is the most renowned and the only one surviving. That of Toledo was gravely damaged in Spain's most recent civil war.

The Hispano-Moslem system of decoration reached its culminating point in the Alhambra. This Acropolis of Granada, with its excessive decoration in mosaics, stalactites and inscriptions, was conceived and constructed on an extensive and magnificent scale. Begun about 1248 by a Nasrid sultan, its construction was completed about the middle of the fourteenth century.

The horseshoe form of arch, which became characteristic of Western Moslem architecture, was represented in the Near East even before Islam. In its round horseshoe variety it was used at the Umayyad Mosque of Damascus. This last type, which in the West became known as the Moorish arch, undoubtedly existed in Spain before the Arab conquest, but it was the Spanish, more particularly the Cordovan, Moslems who realized its structural and decorative possibilities and adopted it generally. Another contribution of Arab Cordova, which was truly original, was the system of vaulting based on intersecting arches and visible intersecting ribs. These and other architectural features developed at Cordova were carried to Toledo and other centers in the north of the peninsula by Mozarabs. Here, by the merging of Christian and Moslem traditions, arose a definite style characterized by almost regular use of the horseshoe arch and the vault. In the hands of Mudejar workmen this

203

mixed art attained great beauty and perfection and became the Spanish national style.

Long after the fall of Granada, Moorish dancers and singers continued to entertain the natives of Spain and Portugal. The recent researches of Ribera tend to show that the popular music of Spain, in fact of all southwestern Europe, in and after the thirteenth century, like the lyric and historical romance of that region, is to be traced to Andalusian and then through Arabic to Persian, Byzantine and Greek sources. Even as philosophy, mathematics and medicine traveled from Greece and Rome to Byzantium, Persia and Baghdad, then to Spain, and thence to all Europe, so did several phases of musical theory and practice.

The only place in Europe, other than Spain, in which the Moslems gained a firm foothold was Sicily. The Moslem conquest of Sicily, which had begun with sporadic raids as early as 652, had been completed in the year 827 and for the next hundred and eighty-nine years Sicily under turbulent Arab chieftains had formed in whole or in part a province of the Arab world. Palermo was its capital.

Just as Spain was a *point d'appui* for further raids and temporary conquests northward, so was Sicily with regard to Italy. Before his death in 902 the amir Ibrahim II, an Aghlabid from Tunisia who also ruled Sicily, had carried the holy war across the straits into the toe of Italy, Calabria, but he was not the first Arab invader to set foot on Italian soil. Shortly after conquering

Palermo other Aghlabid generals from North Africa had interfered in the quarrels of the rival Lombards of Southern Italy, whose heel and toe were still held by the Byzantine emperor, and when Naples in 838 appealed for Arab aid the Moslem war cry echoed on the slopes of Vesuvius. About four years later Bari, on the Adriatic, which was to become the main base for the next thirty years, was captured. About the same time the victorious Moslems made an appearance before Venice. In 846 even Rome was threatened by Arab squadrons which landed at Ostia and, unable to penetrate the walls of the Eternal City, sacked the cathedrals of St. Peter beside the Vatican and of St. Paul outside the walls, and desecrated the graves of the pontiffs. Three years later another Moslem fleet reached Ostia but was destroyed by the tempestuous sea and the Italian navy. A painting from sketches by Raphael recalls this naval fight and the marvelous rescue of Rome. But the hold of the Moslems over Italy remained so firm that Pope John VIII (872-882) deemed it prudent to pay tribute for two years.

The Aghlabids did not limit their operations to the Italian coasts. In 869 they captured Malta. From Italy and Spain piratical raids in the tenth century extended through the Alpine passes into mid-Europe. In the Alps are a number of castles and walls which tourists' guides attribute to the invasion of the Saracens. Certain Swiss place names such as Gaby and Algaby may possibly be of Arabic origin.

The recapture of Bari by the Christians in 871

marks the beginning of the end of the Moslem menace to Italy and Central Europe. In Bari the commanders had gone so far as to declare themselves "sultans" independent of the amir at Palermo. In 880 the Byzantine Emperor Basil I wrested Taranto, another important fortress, from Moslem hands and a few years later expelled the last remnants of Arabs from Calabria. The final stage of the expansion which had begun in distant Arabia two and a half centuries before was thus brought to an end. At the present day numerous "Saracen towers," structures from which the approach of Arab fleets from Sicily or Africa was announced, still contribute to the scenic beauty of the peerless coastline south of Naples.

The Norman conquest of the island of Sicily began with the capture of Messina in 1060 by Count Roger, son of Tancred de Hauteville, culminated in the seizure of Palermo in 1071 and Syracuse in 1085, and ended in 1091. In 1090 Malta was taken by Roger. The Normans, already strong in the possession of a vigorous state on the mainland, were now secure in their newly conquered territory.

Sicily under the Normans saw the appearance of an interesting Christian-Islamic culture. Throughout the Arab period of domination there streamed into the island, already rich in memories of bygone civilizations, Eastern cultural currents which, blending with the precious legacy of Greece and Rome, took definite shape under Norman rule and gave the Norman cul-

SICILY AND SOUTHERN ITALY
To illustrate Moslem occupation

Emery-Walker Ltd.

ture its distinctive character. Hitherto the Arabs had been too engrossed in warfare and quarrels to develop the finer arts of peace, but now their genius attained its full fruition in a rich outburst of Arab-Norman art and culture.

Though himself an uncultured Christian, Roger I drew from the Moslems the mass of his infantry, patronized Arab learning, surrounded himself with Eastern philosophers, astrologers and physicians and allowed the non-Christians full liberty to follow their rites. His court at Palermo seemed more Oriental than Occidental. For over a century after this Sicily presented the unique spectacle of a Christian kingdom in which some of the highest positions were held by Moslems.

The earliest extant document on paper from Europe is an order in Greek and Arabic issued by the wife of Roger I, presumably in 1109. This paper may have been imported by Sicilian Arabs from the East rather than manufactured by them in Sicily.

The strange and fascinating Sicilian-Arab line started by Roger I culminated in his son and successor, Roger II (1130-1154) and in Frederick II. Roger II dressed like a Moslem and his critics called him the "half-heathen king." His robe bore decorative Arabic characters. Even under his grandson a chronicler saw the Christian women of Palermo wearing Moslem costumes.

The chief ornament of Roger II's court was al-Idrisi, the most distinguished geographer and cartographer of the Middle Ages. Born in Ceuta in 1100 of Hispano-Arab parents, abu-Abdullah Muhammad ibn-Muhammad al-Idrisi, who died in 1166, did his lifework at Palermo under the patronage of Roger II. His Rogerian treatise not only sums up the main features of such preceding works as those of Ptolemy and al-Masudi, but is primarily based upon original reports submitted by observers who had been sent to various lands to secure data. In his critical collation of the material al-Idrisi shows a remarkable breadth of view and a grasp of such essential facts as the sphericity of the earth. He located the sources of the Nile, supposedly discovered in the middle nineteenth century, in the equatorial highlands of Africa. Besides this monumental work al-Idrisi constructed for his Norman patron a celestial sphere and a disk-shaped map of the world, both in silver. The second of "the two baptized sultans of Sicily" was Roger II's grandson Frederick II of Hohenstaufen, who ruled both Sicily and Germany and, besides holding the title of emperor of the Holy Roman Empire after 1220, became king of Jerusalem by his marriage in 1225 with the heiress, Isabelle of Brienne. The Emperor Frederick therefore was the highest civil authority in Christendom. Three years after his marriage he undertook a Crusade which indoctrinated him with more Moslem ideas.

In his personal habits and official life Frederick, who kept a harem, was semi-Oriental. In his court flourished philosophers from Syria and Baghdad, with long beards and flowing robes,

dancing girls from the Orient and Jews from the
East as well as from the West. He maintained his
interest in the world of Islam by political and
commercial relations, especially with the sultan
of Egypt. From Egypt he brought experts to test
the incubation of ostrich eggs by the heat of the
sun. From Syria he brought skilled falconers,
watched them train the birds and tried to ascertain by sealing the hawks' eyes whether they
could find food by smell. He had his interpreter-
astrologer Theodore, a Jacobite Christian from
Antioch, translate an Arabic treatise on falconry.
This translation, together with another from
Persian, became the basis of Frederick's work on
falconry, the first modern natural history. As
court astrologer Theodore was preceded by
Michael Scot, who from 1220 to 1236 represented in Sicily and Italy the learning of Moslem
Spain. Scot made for the emperor from Arabic a
Latin summary of Aristotle's biological and zoo-
logical works, with Avicenna's commentary,
which he dedicated to his patron. This almost
modern spirit of investigation, experimentation
and research which characterized the court of
Frederick marks the beginning of the Italian
Renaissance.

But Frederick's greatest single contribution
was the founding of the University of Naples
in 1224, the first in Europe to be established by
a definite charter. In it he deposited a large col-
lection of Arabic manuscripts. The works of
Aristotle and Averroës which he caused to be
translated were used in its curriculum; copies of

the translations were sent to the Universities of
Paris and Bologna. The University of Naples
counted among its pupils Thomas Aquinas. In
the fourteenth and following centuries Arabic
studies were cultivaetd in several European universities, including Oxford and Paris, but with
an entirely different motive: that of preparing
Christian missionaries for Moslem lands.

The meeting point of two cultural areas,
Sicily was peculiarly adapted to act as a medium
for transmitting ancient and medieval lore. Its
population comprised a Greek element which
used Greek, a Moslem element which spoke Arabic and a body of scholars who knew Latin. All
three languages were in current use in the official
registers and royal charters as well as among the
populace of the many-tongued Palermo.

Since the Norman kings and their successors
on the Sicilian throne held not only the island
but also Southern Italy, they provided a bridge
for the transmission of various elements of Moslem culture into the peninsula and mid-Europe.
By the middle of the tenth century traces of
Arab learning became clearly noticeable north
of the Alps. Dante's ideas of the other world may
not have been derived from any particular Arabic text, but they certainly appear to have been
of Oriental origin, though drawn by him from
the popular lore of Europe. This penetration
from the East through various channels is evident in the domain of art as well as in science and
literature. Long after Sicily and the southern
part of the peninsula had reverted to Christian

211

rule, Moslem craftsmen and artists continued to flourish, as evidenced by the mosaics and inscriptions of the Palatine Chapel. The renowned weaving house established by the Moslem rulers in the royal palace at Palermo supplied European royalty with state robes which bore Arabic inscriptions. So great was the demand for Oriental fabrics that there was a time when no European could have felt really well-dressed unless he possessed at least one such garment.

During the fifteenth century, when opulent Venice was so actively adopting and scattering Moslem fashions in art, books bound in Italian workshops began to assume an Oriental appearance. The peculiarities of Arabic binding, including the flap that folds over to protect the front edges of the volume, appear on Christian books. At the same time new methods of tooling and decorating leather covers were also being learned from Oriental artisans in various Italian towns. Venice, moreover, was the home of another Arab craft, the inlaying of brass with gold, silver, or red copper. Sicily, as a transmitter of Moslem culture, might claim for itself a place next in importance to that of Spain and higher than that of Syria in the period of the Crusades.

While the last vestiges of Moslem power were being erased in Europe the caliphate in Baghdad was expiring amid a welter of bloodshed and intrigue. A taste of what was to come and an instance of the way in which it came had been supplied as early as the ninth century by the rise of the Tulunid dynasty, the earliest manifestation

212

of a political crystallization in the unruly and heretofore inarticulate Turkish element in the heart of the caliphate. Other and more important Turkish dynasties were soon to follow. The case of Ahmad ibn-Tulun, who seized power in 868, was typical of the founders of the many states on the ruins of the caliphate. These states broke off entirely from the central government or remained only nominally dependent upon the caliph in Baghdad. Ahmad served as an example of what could be done in the matter of achieving military and political power at the expense of a bulky and unwieldy caliphate through the strong-handed and confident ambition of a subject soldier and his slave satellites. But the Tulunid, and most of the other dynasties, had no national basis in the lands over which they ruled and therefore were short-lived. Their weakness consisted in the absence of a strong coherent body of supporters of their own race. The rulers were themselves intruders who were obliged to recruit their bodyguards, which were their armies, from various alien sources. Such a rule can be maintained only by men of outstanding personal influence and no sooner does the mighty arm of the founder relax than disintegration sets in. The state founded by ibn-Tulun reverted to the Abbasids under his son and fourth successor, in 905.

One separate dynasty lasted for more than two centuries and wrote a page of history which warrants attention—the Fatimid caliphate, the only major Shiite one in Islam, which established itself in Tunis in 909 as a deliberate challenge to the religious headship of the Islamic world represented by the Abbasids of Baghdad. It presently controlled all of North Africa and Egypt and under it the city of Cairo reached a new height of splendor. But for all its wealth at the moment, the Fatimid dynasty was not to endure much longer. The familiar story of intrigue and corruption—plus the precariousness of the existence of the common people, who depended on the overflow of the Nile for sustenance and who were harried by famines, plagues and the not less deadly tax gatherers—undermined its strength. The Fatimid caliphate was overthrown finally in 1171 by the renowned Saladin, in the period of the Crusades.

Politically the Fatimid period marks a new epoch in the history of Egypt, which for the first time since the days of the Pharaohs had a completely sovereign power full of vitality and founded on a religious basis. A Persian missionary traveler who visited the country in 1046-1049 has left us a description in glowing colors. The caliphal palace housed 30,000 persons, of whom 12,000 were servants, and 1,000 horse and foot guards. The young caliph, whom he saw at a festival riding on a mule, was pleasant-looking, clean-shaven and dressed simply in a white caftan and turban. An attendant carried over the caliph's head a parasol enriched with precious stones. The seven galleys drawn up on the bank of the Nile measured 150 cubits over-all by 60 in beam. The caliph owned in the capital 20,000 houses, mostly of brick, rising to a height of five or six stories, and an equal number of shops, which were let at two to ten dinars a month. The main streets were roofed and lighted by lamps. The shopkeepers sold at fixed prices, and if one cheated he was paraded on a camel through the streets ringing a bell and confessing his fault. Even the shops of jewelers and money-changers were left unlocked. The whole country enjoyed a degree of seeming tranquillity and prosperity that made the missionary enthusiastically declare: "I could neither limit nor estimate its wealth and nowhere have I seen such prosperity as I saw there."

While the Fatimids were ruling in Egypt and North Africa, disintegration was proceeding rapidly in the heart of the old empire at Baghdad. The Saljuq Turks enjoyed a period of ascendancy and put one of their number, Tughril, as ruler in the caliph's capital in the year 1037. As fresh Turkish tribesmen swelled their armies, the Saljuqs extended their conquests in all directions until once more Western Asia was united into one Moslem kingdom and the fading glory of Moslem arms revived. A new race from Central Asia was pouring its blood into the struggle of Islam for world supremacy. The story of these barbarian infidels, setting their feet on the necks of the followers of the Prophet and at the same time accepting the religion of the conquered and becoming its ardent champions, was not unique in the checkered annals of that religion. Their cousins, the Mongols of the thirteenth century, as well as their other kinsmen, the Ottoman Turks of the early fourteenth century, repeated the same process. In the darkest hour of political Islam religious Islam proved able to achieve some of its most brilliant victories.

The hour was dark indeed for Islam now. In 1216 Jenghiz Khan, with an appalling swarm of some sixty thousand Mongolian barbarians, riding fleet horses and armed with strange bows, appeared to spread havoc and destruction. Before them the cultural centers of eastern Islam were practically wiped out of existence, leaving bare deserts or shapeless ruins where formerly had stood stately palaces and libraries. A crimson streak marked their trail. Out of a population of 100,000, Herat was left with 40,000. The mosques of Bukhara, famed for piety and learning, served as stables for Mongolian horses. Many of the inhabitants of Samarqand and Balkh were either butchered or carried into captivity. Khwarizm was utterly devastated. Baghdad's turn was soon to come. At the capture of Bukhara, Jenghiz is reported by a late tradition to have described himself in a speech as "the scourge of God sent to men as a punishment for their sins." The people he led had by the first half of the thirteenth century shaken every kingdom from China to the Adriatic. Russia was in part overrun and central Europe penetrated as far as eastern Prussia. It was only the death of Jenghiz's son and successor in 1241 that saved Western Europe from these Mongolian hordes. There was no salvation for Baghdad.

The Cross Supplants the Crescent

In 1253 Hulagu, a grandson of Jenghiz Khan, left Mongolia at the head of a huge army intent upon the destruction of the caliphate. The second wave of Mongol hordes was on. It swept before it all those petty princedoms which were striving to grow on the ruins of the empire. In January 1258 the mangonels of Hulagu were in effective operation against the walls of the capital. Soon a breach was effected in one of the towers. The vizir, accompanied by the Nestorian primate—Hulagu had a Christian wife—appeared to ask for terms. But Hulagu refused to receive them. Equally ineffective were warnings citing the fate of others who had dared to violate "the city of peace" or undo the Abbasid caliphate. Hulagu was told that "if the caliph is killed the whole universe is disorganized, the sun hides its face, rain ceases and plants grow no more." But he knew better, thanks to the advice of his astrologers. By the tenth of February his hordes had swarmed into the city and the unfortunate caliph with his three hundred officials rushed to offer an unconditional surrender. Ten days later they were all put to death. The city itself was given over to plunder and flames; the majority of its population, including the family of the caliph, were wiped out of existence. Pestilential odors emitted by corpses strewn unburied in the streets compelled Hulagu to withdraw from the town for a few days. But as he intended to retain Baghdad for his residence the devastation was not as thorough as in other towns. The Nestorian patriarch received special favors. Certain schools and mosques were spared or rebuilt. For the first time in its history the Moslem world was left without a caliph whose name could be cited in the Friday prayers.

In 1260 Hulagu was threatening northern Syria. Here he captured Hamah and Harim in addition to Aleppo, where he put to the sword some fifty thousand people. After dispatching a general to the siege of Damascus he felt himself constrained by the death of his brother, the Great Khan, to return to Persia. The army left behind, after subjugating Syria, was destroyed in 1260 near Nazareth by Baybars, the distinguished general of the last medieval dynasty of the Arab world, the Mamluks.

Hulagu, the first to assume the title of Il-Khan, died in 1265. Less than half a century after his death the faith of Muhammad scored another of its dazzling victories when the seventh Khan recognized Islam as the state religion. Just as in the case of the Saljuqs, the religion of the Moslems conquered the Mongols where their arms had failed.

Meanwhile, on a front farther west, Islam had been undergoing another assault, one which wrote one of the memorable pages in the history of our own civilization and which saw the rise of one of Islam's greatest champions. This was the period of the Crusades, and of Salah-al-Din —Saladin.

The Crusades

The Crusades represent the medieval chapter in the long story of interaction between East and West. The Trojan and Persian wars of antiquity were the prelude and the imperialistic expansion of modern Western Europe was the latest chapter.

More specifically, the Crusades represent the reaction of Christian Europe against Moslem Asia, which had been on the offensive since 632 not only in Syria and Asia Minor but in Spain and Sicily also. Among other antecedents were the migratory and military tendencies of the Teutonic tribes, who had changed the map of Europe since their entrance into the light of history; the destruction by a Fatimid caliph in 1009 of the Church of the Holy Sepulchre—the object of pilgrimage for thousands of Europeans and whose keys had been sent in 800 to Charlemagne as a blessing by the patriarch of Jerusalem —and the hardships to which pilgrims through Moslem Asia Minor were subjected. The immediate cause of the Crusades, however, was the repeated appeal made in 1095 to Pope Urban II by the Byzantine Emperor Alexius Comnenus, whose Asiatic possessions had been overrun by the Saljuqs as far as the shores of Marmora. These Moslems threatened Constantinople itself. The Pope possibly viewed the appeal as affording an opportunity for reuniting the Greek Church and Rome, the final schism between the two having been effected between 1009 and 1054.

Probably the most effective speech in all history was made when, on November 26, 1095, Pope Urban spoke at Clermont in southeastern France, urging the faithful to "enter upon the road to the Holy Sepulchre, wrest it from the wicked race and subject it" to themselves. The rallying cry "God wills it!" ran through the land and seized high and low with its psychical contagion. By the spring of the following year a hundred and fifty thousand men, mostly Franks and Normans, had answered the call and met at Constantinople. The first of the Crusades, so called from the cross borne as a badge, had started.

Not all, of course, who took the cross were actuated by spiritual motives. Several of the leaders, including Bohemond, were intent upon acquiring principalities for themselves. The merchants of Pisa, Venice and Genoa had commercial interests. The romantic, the restless and the adventurous, in addition to the devout, found a new rallying point and many criminals sought penance thereby. To the great mass of the inhabitants of France, Lorraine, Italy and Sicily, with their depressed economic and social conditions, taking the cross was a relief rather than a sacrifice.

The customary classification into a definite number of Crusades, seven to nine, is by no means satisfactory. The stream was more or less continuous and the line of demarcation between Crusades not sharply drawn. A more logical division would be into, first, a period of conquest extending to 1144; second, a period of Moslem reaction culminating in the brilliant victories of Saladin; and third, a period of civil and petty wars ending in 1291 when the Crusaders lost their last foothold on the Syrian mainland. The period of conquest falls in its entirety before the so-called Second Crusade, 1147-1149, and the third period coincides roughly with the thirteenth century. One of the Crusades of this last period was directed against Constantinople, 1202-1204, two against Egypt, 1218-1221, accomplishing nothing, and one even to Tunisia in 1270.

The route of the first Crusaders from their rendezvous at Constantinople lay across Asia Minor. This victorious march restored to Alexius, who had exacted from almost all the Crusading leaders an oath of feudal allegiance, the western half of the peninsula and helped to delay the

Turkish invasion of Europe for three centuries
and a half.

First Edessa, then Tarsus, Antioch and Aleppo
fell to the invaders, all in 1098. The discovery of
the "holy lance," which had pierced the Sav-
iour's side as He hung upon the cross and had
lain buried in a church in Antioch, gave fresh en-
thusiasm to the invaders. On June 7, 1099, some
forty thousand Crusaders, of whom about
twenty thousand were effective troops, stood before the gates of Jerusalem. The Egyptian garrison may be estimated at about one thousand.
Hoping the walls would fall as those of Jericho
had done, the Crusaders first marched barefoot
around the city, blowing their horns. A month's
siege proved more effective. On July 15 the besiegers stormed the city and perpetrated an in-
discriminate massacre involving all ages and both
sexes. "Heaps of heads and hands and feet were
to be seen throughout the streets and squares of
the city." Many of the Crusaders and pilgrims,
considering their vows now fulfilled, sailed back
home.

Under the leadership of Raymond of Toulouse, the most powerful count of France, Bohemond, Baldwin, Godfrey and Tancred, the Crusading army had set up three small Latin states,
in Syria-Palestine, and others were to be established. But they were not long to endure, and
their history of squabbles and petty rivalries
forms a chapter of European rather than of Arab
history. But the peaceful and friendly relations

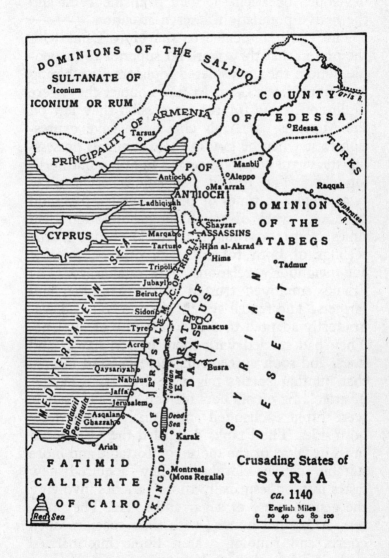

DOMINIONS OF THE SALJUQ

SULTANATE OF
○ Iconium
ICONIUM OR RUM

COUNTY
OF EDESSA

○ Edessa

TURKS

PRINCIPALITY OF ARMENIA

Tarsus ○

ALBISUL
Tigris R.

P. OF
ANTIOCH

Antioch ○

Manbij ●
Aleppo ○
○ Ma'arrah

Raqqah ●

Euphrates R.

Ladhiqiyah ○

Shayzar ○
Marqab ○ ◄ ASSASSINS
Tartus ○ Hisn al-Akrad ○
Hims ○

DOMINION
OF THE
ATABEGS

CYPRUS

Tripoli ○

○ Tadmur

MEDITERRANEAN SEA

Jubayl ○
Beirut ○

Sidon ○

Tyre ○

Damascus ●

Acre ○

Qaysariyah ○

Busra ●

Nabulus ○
Jaffa ○

Jerusalem ○

Asqalan ○
Ghazzah ○

Barriawil Peninsula

Dead Sea

Arish ○

Karak ○

SYRIAN DESERT

FATIMID
CALIPHATE
OF CAIRO

Red Sea

Montreal ○
(Mons Regalis)

JERUSALEM

COUNTY OF TRIPOLI

EMIRATE OF DAMASCUS

Jordan R.

KINGDOM OF

Crusading States of
SYRIA
ca. 1140

English Miles
0   20   40   60   80   100

developed between the men from the West and the native population deserve attention.

The Christians came to the Holy Land with the notion that they were far superior to its people, whom they considered idolaters, worshiping Muhammad as a God. At first contact they were disillusioned. As for the impression they left on the Moslems, an Arab chronicler gave expression to it when he saw in them "animals possessing the virtues of courage and fighting, but nothing else." The forced association between the two peoples in times of peace—which, it should be noted, were of much longer duration than times of war—wrought a radical change in the feelings of both toward each other. Amicable and neighborly relations were established. The Franks employed trusted native workmen and farmers. The feudal system they introduced was gradually adapted to the local tenure of the land. They had carried with them horses, hawks and dogs, and soon agreements were entered into so that hunting parties might be free from danger of attack. Safe-conducts for travelers and traders were often exchanged and usually honored by both sides. The Franks discarded their European dress in favor of the more comfortable and more suitable native clothing. They acquired new tastes in food, especially those varieties involving the generous use of sugar and spices. They preferred Oriental houses, with their spacious open courts and running water. Some intermarried with natives and the half-caste progeny of native mothers were designated as *poulains*—"kids," or "young ones." They even in certain instances venerated shrines held equally sacred by Moslems and Jews. In their intermittent quarrels among themselves the Latins often welcomed assistance from the "infidels," and the Moslems often sought alliances with Latins against fellow Moslems.

The reaction to the Christian conquest of Syria and much of Egypt, which began to make itself felt about 1127, brought to the center of the stage the romantic figure of Saladin—al-Malik al-Nasir al-Sultan Salah-al-Din Yusuf (the defending king, the Sultan, the Bounty of Religion, Joseph—as his correct name was), a Syrian of Kurdish parentage, vizir of Egypt in 1169, who had dedicated himself to the banishment of Shiite doctrines in Egypt and to the pressing of the holy war against the Franks.

On July 1, 1187, he captured Tiberias after a six days' siege. The battle of the adjacent Hittin followed. It began on Friday, the day of prayer and a favorite one with Saladin for fighting. This was a sad day for the Franks. Numbering about twenty thousand and all but dying of thirst and heat, their army fell almost in its entirety into the enemy's hands. The list of distinguished captives was headed by Guy de Lusignan, king of Jerusalem. The chivalrous sultan gave the crestfallen monarch a friendly reception; but his companion, Reginald of Chatillon, merited a different treatment. Reginald was perhaps the most adventurous and least scrupulous of all the Latin leaders and the most facile in the use of Arabic.

Entrusted with the command of the city of
Karak, Latinized into Crac, he more than once
fell upon peaceful caravans and plundered them
as they passed beneath the walls of his castle—
and that in violation of treaty relations. He even
fitted out a fleet and harassed the coasts of the
sacred territory of Hijaz, preying upon its pilgrims. Saladin had sworn to slay with his own
hand the breaker of truce, and now the time
came for the fulfillment of his oath. Taking advantage of a recognized tradition connected
with Arab hospitality, Reginald secured a drink
of water from his captor's tent. But the drink was
not offered by Saladin and therefore established
no guest and host relationship between captive
and captor. Reginald paid for his treachery with
his life. All the Templars and Hospitallers were
also publicly executed.

The victory of Hittin sealed the fate of the
Frankish cause. After a week's siege Jerusalem,
which had lost its garrison at Hittin, capitulated
on October 2, 1187. In the Aqsa Mosque the
muezzin's call replaced the Christian gong, and
the golden cross which surmounted the Dome of
the Rock was torn down by Saladin's men.

The capture of the capital of the Latin kingdom gave Saladin most of the towns of Frankish
Syria-Palestine. In a series of brilliantly executed
campaigns, most of the remaining strongholds
were seized. The Franks came very near being
swept out of the land. Only Antioch, Tripoli and
Tyre, besides certain smaller towns and castles,
remained in their possession.

The Crusades

The fall of the holy city aroused Europe. Hostilities among its rulers were buried. Frederick Barbarossa, emperor of Germany, Richard Coeur de Lion, king of England, and Philip Augustus, king of France, took the cross. These three were the most powerful sovereigns of Western Europe, and with them the "Third Crusade," 1189-1192, began. In point of numbers it was one of the largest. For legend and romance, both Oriental and Occidental, this Crusade, with Saladin and Coeur de Lion as its chief figures, has provided the favorite theme.

Frederick, who was the first to start, took the land route and was drowned while crossing a Cilician river. Most of his followers returned home. En route Richard stopped to capture Cyprus, destined to become the last refuge of the Crusaders driven from the mainland.

In the meantime the Latins in the Holy Land had decided that Acre provided the key to the restoration of their lost domain. Against it they marched virtually all their forces, augmented by the remnant of Frederick's army and the contingents of the king of France. King Guy, who had been released by Saladin on pledging his honor never again to bear arms against him, led the attack. Saladin arrived the next day to rescue the city and pitched his camp facing the enemy. The struggle was waged by land and sea. The arrival of Richard was hailed with great rejoicing and bonfires. During the progress of the siege many picturesque incidents took place and were recorded by the contemporary Arabic and

227

Latin chroniclers. Saladin and Richard even exchanged presents, but never met. Richard offered a handsome reward for every stone dislodged from the walls of the city, and the combatants, as well as the women, performed deeds of great valor. The siege, considered one of the major military operations of medieval times, dragged on for two years—August 27, 1189 to July 12, 1191. The Franks had the advantage of a fleet and up-to-date siege artillery; the Moslems had the advantage of single command. Finally the garrison surrendered.

Two of the conditions of surrender were the release of the garrison on the payment of 200,-000 gold pieces and the restoration of the holy Cross. When at the end of a month the money was not paid, Richard ordered the twenty-seven hundred captives to be slaughtered—an act that stands in conspicuous contrast with Saladin's treatment of his prisoners at the capture of Jerusalem. He too had then stipulated a ransom and several thousand of the poor could not redeem themselves. At the request of his brother, however, Saladin had set free a thousand of these poor captives; at the request of the patriarch another group was released. Then, considering that his brother and the patriarch had made their alms and that his own turn had come, Saladin freed without ransom many of the remaining captives, including numerous women and children.

Acre now takes the place of Jerusalem in leadership and henceforth negotiations for peace be-

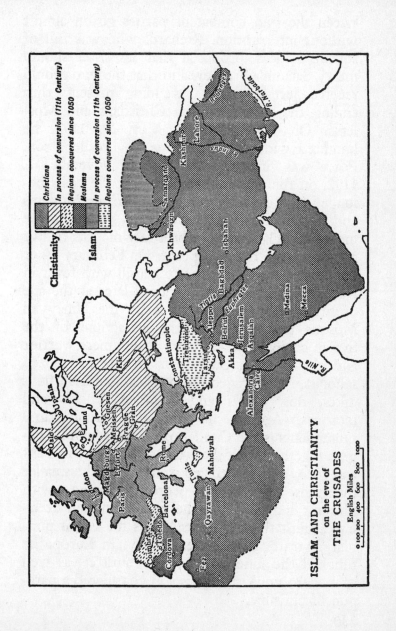

ISLAM AND CHRISTIANITY
on the eve of
THE CRUSADES

English Miles
0 100 200 400 600 800 1000

Christianity
Christians
In process of conversion (11th Century)
Regions conquered since 1050

Islam
Moslems
In process of conversion (11th Century)
Regions conquered since 1050

Oslo
Upsala
London
Makdeburg
Paris
Gnesen
Erfurt
Meissen
Prague
Gran
Rome
Toledo
Coimbra
Cordova
Barcelona
Tunis
Mahdiyah
Qayrawān
Fez
Kiev
Constantinople
Trebizond
Tarsus
Tarsus
Alexandria
Cairo
Beirut
Akka
Ascalon
Jerusalem
Aleppo
Baghdad
Tigris
Euphrates
Medina
Mecca
Isbahan
Khwārizm
Samarqand
Kashmir
Lahore
R. Ganges
R. Indus
R. Nile
R. Volga

tween the two combatant parties go on almost
without interruption. Richard, who was full of
romantic ideas, proposed that his sister should
marry Saladin's brother, and that the two should
receive Jerusalem as a wedding present, thus
ending the strife between Christians and Moslems. On Palm Sunday, May 29, 1192, he
knighted with full ceremony his brother's son.
Peace was finally concluded on November 2,
1192, on the general principle that the coast belonged to the Latins, the interior to the Moslems
and that pilgrims to the holy city should not be
molested. Saladin had only a few months to live
and enjoy the fruits of peace. On February 19 of
the following year he was taken ill with fever in
Damascus and died twelve days later at the age
of fifty-five. His tomb close by the Umayyad
Mosque is still one of the attractions of the
Syrian capital. He was more than a mere warrior
and champion of Sunnite Islam. He patronized
scholars, encouraged theological studies, built
dikes, dug canals and founded schools and
mosques. Among his surviving architectural
monuments is the Citadel of Cairo, which he began, together with the walls of the city, in 1183
and for which he utilized stones from the smaller
pyramids. Among his people his name, with
Harun's and Baybars', the next champion of Islam against the Crusaders, heads the list of popular favorites to the present day. In Europe he
touched the fancy of English minstrels as well
as modern novelists and is still considered a para-
gon of chivalry.

The sporadic fighting which went on during almost a century following, with inconclusive results save that the Latins more or less maintained their position, was noteworthy only for the events of the "Sixth Crusade," that of Louis IX of France, and his chevaliers. This king, the St. Louis of history, in 1249 captured the city of Dimyat in Egypt; but as his army marched on Cairo, in a marshy region intersected by canals, while the Nile was at its height, pestilence spread in its ranks, its line of communication was cut off and it was entirely destroyed. King Louis, with most of his nobles, was taken prisoner. After a month of captivity they were released on the payment of a ransom and the restoration of the city of Dimyat. In 1270 Louis led another futile Crusade, this time to Tunisia, where he died. Of all the Crusading leaders his character was by far the noblest.

It was Baybars, of the strange slave dynasty of Egypt, the Mamluks, who inaugurated the series of sultans who dealt the final blows to the Crusaders' cause. In 1263 he occupied Karak and demolished the venerated church of Nazareth. Caesarea, Jaffa, Antioch fell to his irresistible and merciless assaults. Antioch's garrison, to the number of 16,000, was slaughtered, and some 100,000, men and women, boys and girls, taken and sold as slaves. When the plunder was divided, money was measured out in cups; an infant fetched twelve dirhams and a young girl five. Antioch never recovered from the pillage.

Under Baybars' successors Acre was besieged,

ninety-two catapults leveled against its ramparts, and its walls stormed in 1291. Its Templar defenders were massacred. Tyre, Sidon, Beirut and Antartus were occupied in the same year. The Crusaders were driven into the sea; one of the most dramatic chapters in the history of Syria was closed.

Because of the richness of the Crusades in picturesque and romantic incidents, their historical importance has been somewhat exaggerated. For the Occident they meant much more than for the Orient. Their civilizing influence was artistic, industrial and commercial rather than scientific and literary. In Syria they left in their wake havoc and ruin and throughout the Near East they bequeathed a legacy of ill will between Moslems and Christians that has not yet been forgotten.

In the epoch of the Crusades Moslem culture was already decadent in the East. In philosophy, medicine, music and other disciplines its great lights had almost all vanished. This partly explains why Syria, which was throughout the twelfth and thirteenth centuries a particular focus of relations between Islam and Western Christianity, proved to be a vehicle of Arabic influence very much less important than either Spain, Sicily, North Africa or even the Byzantine empire. Although in Syria Islam acted upon European Christianity by direct impact upon the Crusaders, by the repercussion of that impact upon the West and by a process of infiltration along the routes of commerce, yet the spiritual

232

and intellectual impress it left is barely notice-able. On the other hand, we should recall that the Franks in Syria, besides possessing a lower level of culture than their antagonists, were largely foreign legions quartered in castles and barracks and in close contact with the native tillers of the soil and artisans rather than with the intelligentsia. Then there were the nationalis-tic and religious prejudices and animosities which thwarted the play of interactive forces. In science and art the Franks had very little to teach the natives. The comparative standing of medical lore in the two camps may be illustrated by the anecdotes cleverly told by a contem-porary Arab chronicler who also pokes fun at the Frank's judicial procedure with its trial by duel and by water.

Since in the twelfth century we find a num-ber of hospices and hospitals, chiefly lazar houses for leprosy, springing up all over Europe, we may assume that the idea of systematic hospitali-zation received a stimulus from the Moslem Ori-ent. This Orient was also responsible for the re-introduction into Europe of public baths, an in-stitution which the Romans patronized but the Christians discouraged.

In literature the influence was more pervasive. The legends of the Holy Grail have elements of undoubted Syrian origin. The Crusaders must have heard stories from the Bidpai fables and the *Arabian Nights* and carried them back with them. Chaucer's *Squieres Tale* is an *Arabian Nights* story. From oral sources Boccaccio derived the Oriental tales incorporated in his *Decameron.* To the Crusaders we may also ascribe European missionary interest in Arabic and other Islamic languages.

In the realm of warfare the influences, as is to be expected, are more noticeable. The use of the crossbow, the wearing of heavy mail by knight and horse and the use of cotton pads under the armor are of Crusading origin. In Syria the Franks adopted the tabor (corrupted from an Arabic word) and the drum for their military bands, which hitherto had been served only by trumpets and horns. They learned from the natives how to train carrier pigeons to convey military information, and borrowed from them the practice of celebrating victory by illuminations and the knightly sport of the tournament. In fact certain important features of the institution of chivalry developed on the plains of Syria. The growing use of armorial bearings and heraldic devices was due to contact with Moslem knights.

The Crusades also fostered the improvement of siege tactics, including the art of sapping and mining, the employment of mangonels and battering rams and the application of various combustibles and explosives. Gunpowder was evidently invented in China, where it was used exclusively as an incendiary and whence it was introduced into Europe by the Mongols. The application of its explosive force to the propulsion of missiles, i.e. the invention of firearms, which was by far the more important step, was

234

accomplished in Europe in the second quarter of the fourteenth century. The first European recipe for gunpowder we find appended to a work written about 1300 by a certain Marc the Greek; Bacon's recipe is apocryphal.

In the realm of agriculture, industry and commerce the Crusades produced much greater results than in the realm of the intellect. They explain the popularization in the regions of the Western Mediterranean of such new plants and crops as sesame and carob, millet and rice, lemons and melons, apricots and shallots. "Carob" is Arab *kharrub;* lemon is Arabic *laymun,* of Indic or Malay origin; and both "shallot" and "scallion," meaning originally the onion of Ascalon, preserve the name of the Palestinian town. For many years apricots were called the plums of Damascus.

During their stay in the Orient, the Franks acquired new tastes, especially in perfumes, spices, sweetmeats and other tropical products of Arabia and India with which the marts of Syria were well stocked. These tastes later supported the commerce of Italian and Mediterranean cities. Incense and other fragrant gums of Arabia, the damask rose and sweet scents in which Damascus specialized, and numerous fragrant volatile oils and attars of Persia became favorites. Alum and aloes figured among the new drugs with which they became acquainted. Cloves and other aromatic spices together with pepper and similar condiments came into use in the Occident in the twelfth century, and from that time on no banquet was complete without spiced dishes. Ginger (an Arabic word) was added to the Crusaders' menu in Egypt. More important than all other is sugar, the Arabic *sukkar*. Europeans had hitherto used honey for sweetening their foods. On the maritime plain of Syria-Lebanon, where children can still be seen sucking sugar cane, the Franks became acquainted with this plant which has since played such an important role in our domestic economy and medical prescriptions. Sugar was the first luxury introduced into the West and nothing else so delighted the Western palate. With it went soft drinks, waters tinctured by distillation with roses, violets or other flowers, and all varieties of candy (of Arabic etymology) and sweetmeats. Fabrics such as muslin, damask, atlas and satin were introduced from the Arab East as their names indicate.

The creation of a new European market for Oriental agricultural products and industrial commodities, together with the necessity of transporting pilgrims and Crusaders, stimulated maritime activity and international trade to an extent unknown since Roman days. Marseille began to rival the Italian city republics as a shipping center and share in the increasing wealth. The financial needs of the new situation necessitated a larger supply and a more rapid circulation of money. A system of credit notes was thereupon devised. Firms of bankers arose in Genoa and Pisa with branch offices in the Levant. The Templars began to use letters of credit, receive money on deposit and lend at interest.

An important invention connected with this maritime activity of the Crusades is the compass. The Chinese were probably the first to discover the directive property of the magnetic needle, but the Moslems, who very early carried on lively trade between the Persian Gulf and Far Eastern waters, were the first to make practical use of that discovery by applying the needle to navigation. This discovery they now passed on to the West.

Throughout this period, the Arab empire was contracting and the Moslem mind hardening; but the European man was opening his eyes to a dramatically expanded world. Before the expiration of that empire, however, a last attempt at its revival was made by the Syro-Egyptian Mamluk dynasty.

The Last Dynasty

The last medieval dynasty of the Arab world, the Mamluk, was the most extraordinary. In other than Moslem annals the rise and prosperity of such a dynasty is hardly conceivable. The Mamluks were a dynasty of slaves—the word Mamluk means "possessed"—, slaves of varied races and nationalities forming a military oligarchy in an alien land. They are noteworthy not only because they were, in a sense, the logical climax of the corruption in Arab social life which had been in process for centuries but also because of their real achievements. These slave sultans deserve a page in the closing history of the Arab empire.

They cleared their Syrian-Egyptian domain of the remnant of the Crusaders. They checked forever the advance of the redoubtable Mongol

hordes of Hulagu and of Timur, who might
otherwise have changed the entire course of history and culture in Western Asia and Egypt. Because of this check Egypt was spared the devastation that befell Syria and Iraq and enjoyed a
continuity in culture and political institutions
which no other Moslem land outside Arabia enjoyed. For about two and three-quarter centuries, 1250-1517, the Mamluks dominated one of
the most turbulent areas of the world, keeping
themselves all the while racially distinct. Though
on the whole uncultured and blood-thirsty, their
keen appreciation of art and architecture would
have been a credit to any civilized dynasty and
makes Cairo even now one of the beauty spots
of the Moslem world. And finally, when they
were overthrown in 1517 by the Ottoman Salim,
the last of the petty dynasties that had developed
on the ruins of the Arab caliphate expired, clearing the way for the establishment of a new and
non-Arab caliphate, that of the Ottoman Turks.

The most distinguished of Mamluk sultans and
the real founder of Mamluk power was Baybars.
The petty dynasty which ruled Egypt had followed the precedent of the earlier caliphs of
Baghdad in taking foreign slaves into their services as a bodyguard, with the same eventual result. The bondmen, more capable and vigorous
than their masters, became the army commanders and then the sultans. Baybars, originally a
Turkish slave, was made leader of a section of
the sultan's bodyguard, and from that position
worked his way to the highest place in Egypt.

239

He did so, of course, by bloodshed and violence, but in terms of the decadent Arab world he took the "career open to talent." In this Mamluk dynasty there was no principle of succession and no pretense of one; the strongest survived—but for almost three centuries the strongest were slaves or the descendants of slaves. Baybars himself was tall, dusky in complexion, commanding in voice, brave and energetic—possessed of genuine qualities of leadership.

He won his first laurels against the Mongols in Palestine, but his title to fame rests mainly on his numerous campaigns against the Crusaders. It was these campaigns, as we have noted, which broke the backbone of Frankish opposition. In the meantime his generals had extended his dominion westward over the Berbers and southward over Nubia, which was now permanently controlled by an Egyptian sultan.

Baybars was more than a military leader. Not only did he organize the army, rebuild the navy and strengthen the fortresses of Syria, but he dug canals, improved harbors and connected Cairo and Damascus by a swift postal service requiring only four days. Relays of horses stood in readiness at each post station. The sultan could play polo in both capitals almost within the same week. Besides the ordinary mail the Mamluks perfected the pigeon post, whose carriers even under the Fatimids had their pedigrees kept in special registers. Baybars fostered public works, beautiful mosques and established religious and charitable endowments. Of his architectural

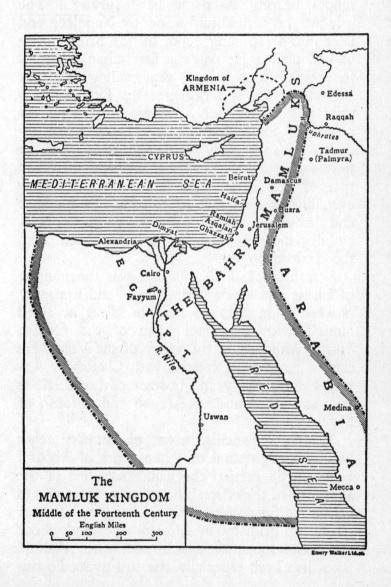

Kingdom of
ARMENIA

○ Edessa

Raqqah ○

Euphrates

Tadmur
○ (Palmyra)

CYPRUS

MEDITERRANEAN   SEA

Beirut○   Damascus

Haifa○   ○Busra

Ramlah○   ○Jerusalem
Asqalan○
Ghazzah○

Dimyat○

Alexandria○

E
G
Y
P
T

Cairo○

Fayyum○

THE   BAHRI   MAMLUKS

A
R
A
B
I
A

R. Nile

R
E
D

S
E
A

Medina ○

Uswan○

Mecca ○

The
MAMLUK KINGDOM
Middle of the Fourteenth Century
English Miles

○   50   100   200   300

Emery Walker Ltd. sc.

monuments both the great mosque and the school bearing his name have survived. The mosque was turned into a fort by Napoleon and later into a rationing depot by the British army of occupation. He was the first sultan in Egypt to appoint four judges, representing the four orthodox rites, and organize the Egyptian pilgrimage to Mecca on a systematic and permanent basis. His religious orthodoxy and zeal, together with the glory he brought to Islam in the holy war, combined to make his name a rival to that of Harun. In legendary history it looms even higher than that of Saladin. His romance and that of pre-Islamic Antar remain to the present day more popular in the Arab Orient than the *Arabian Nights.*

A feature of Baybars' reign was the number of alliances he made with Mongol and European powers. Soon after he became sultan he allied himself with the chief khan of the Golden Horde, Mongols, in the valley of the Volga. He signed commercial treaties with Charles of Anjou, king of Sicily and brother of Louis IX, as well as with James of Aragon and Alfonso of Seville.

A most spectacular event of Baybars' reign was his inauguration of a new series of Abbasid caliphs who carried the name but none of the authority of the office. The sultan's object was to confer legitimacy upon his crown, give his court an air of primacy in Moslem eyes and check the (Shiite intrigues) which, ever since Fatimid days, had been especially rife in Egypt. To this

end he invited from Damascus in June 1261 an
uncle of the last Abbasid caliph who had escaped the Baghdad massacre, and installed him
with great pomp and ceremony. The would-be
pensioner-caliph was first escorted from Syria in
state, with even Jews and Christians carrying
aloft the Torah and the Gospel, and the sound-
ness of his genealogy was passed upon by a council of jurists. The sultan in turn received from
his puppet caliph a diploma of investiture giving him authority over Egypt, Syria, Hijaz, Yaman and the land of the Euphrates. Three months
later Baybars rashly set out from Cairo to rees-
tablish his caliph in Baghdad, but after reaching
Damascus abandoned him to his fate. The hapless
puppet was attacked in the desert by the Mongol
governor of Baghdad and never heard from
again, but one such caliph after another, for two
and a half centuries, held the pseudo-caliphate,
whose incumbents were satisfied with having
their names inscribed on the coinage and mentioned in the Friday prayers in Egypt and Syria.
When in 1517 the Ottoman Sultan Salim
wrested Egypt from the Mamluks he carried
away with him to Constantinople the Caliph al-
Mutawakkil, the last of the line.

Egypt began its history under proud and triumphant rulers who had cleared Syria of the last
vestiges of Frankish dominion and had success-
fully stood between the Mongols and world
power. By the end of the period, however, with
its military oligarchy, factions among the dominant caste, debased coinage, high taxation, inse-

curity of life and property, occasional plague and famine and frequent revolts, both Egypt and its dependency Syria were all but ruined. Especially in the valley of the Nile, superstition and magic were prevalent, coupled with the triumph of reactionary orthodoxy. Under these conditions no intellectual activity of high order could be expected. In fact the whole Arab world had by the beginning of the thirteenth century lost the intellectual hegemony it had maintained since the eighth. Mental fatigue induced by generations of effort and moral lassitude consequent upon the accumulation of wealth and power were evident everywhere.

In science there were only two branches wherein the Arabs after the middle of the thirteenth century maintained their leadership: astronomy-mathematics, including trigonometry, and medicine, particularly ophthalmology. In medicine the name that stands out is that of ibn-al-Nafis who studied in Damascus, where he died in 1289 after serving as dean of a hospital in Cairo. Ibn-al-Nafis contributed a clear conception of the circulation of the blood three centuries before the Portuguese Servetus, who is credited with this discovery. The period was especially fertile in works half gynecological, half erotic, of the type we now designate "sex books." Arabic literature, in all ages primarily a male literature, abounds in anecdotes, jokes and remarks which to us today sound obscene.

The most pleasant surprise of the Mamluk period, dominated by a regime of blood and iron,

is an extraordinary architectural and artistic pro-
ductivity on a scale and of a quality without
parallel in Egyptian history since Ptolemaic and
Pharaonic days. The Mamluk school of architecture received fresh Syro-Mesopotamian influences when in the thirteenth century Egypt became a haven of refuge for Moslem artists and
artisans who fled from Mosul, Baghdad and
Damascus before the Mongol invasions. With
the ending of the Crusades, access to the stone-
building territory to the north was gained once
more, and brick was abandoned in minaret construction in favor of stone. The cruciform plan
of school-mosque structure was developed to its
perfection. Domes were constructed that defy
rivalry for lightness, beauty of outline and richness of decoration. Striped masonry and decoration, obtained by using stones of different colors
in alternate courses, of Roman or Byzantine
origin, became a feature. The period was also
noteworthy for the development of the stalactite
pendentive as well as for the two other familiar
features of Moslem decoration; geometrical
arabesques and Kufic lettering (throughout all
the Moslem ages animal forms were less freely
used in Egypt and Syria than in Spain and Persia). Happily, the finest examples of Mamluk
structures have survived and still form one of the
main attractions for tourists and scholars alike.

By the end of the fourteenth century the story
of the Mamluks became one of the darkest in
Syro-Egyptian annals. Several of the sultans were
treacherous and bloodthirsty, some were ineffi-

cient or even degenerate, most of them were uncultured. From 1412 to 1421 the sultan was a
drunkard who had been bought from a Cir-
cassian dealer. He committed some of the worst
excesses. Another was not familiar with Arabic.
He had his two physicians beheaded because
they could give him no relief from a fatal malady.
The one who ruled in 1453 could neither read
nor write. His name on the official documents he
traced over the writing of a secretary. Nor was
he above suspicion in the matter of pederasty,
with which Baybars, among other Mamluks, was
charged; the *ghilman* institution of Abbasid
notoriety was flourishing under the Mamluks. A
successor was not only illiterate but insane. Another, who had been purchased for fifty dinars,
had an alchemist blinded and deprived of his
tongue for his failure to turn dross into gold.

The evil economic situation of the kingdom
was aggravated by the selfish policy of the sultans. One of them, for example, forbade the importation of spices from India, including the
much desired pepper, and before the price rose
cornered the existing supply and sold it to his
subjects at a great profit. He also monopolized
the manufacture of sugar and went so far as to
prohibit the planting of sugar cane for a period
in order to realize excessive profits for himself.
In his reign another of the periodic plagues
visited Egypt and neighboring countries, and
sugar was in special demand as a remedy against
the disease. Though not quite as devastating as
the "black death," this epidemic is said to have

carried away in the capital alone 300,000 victims within three months. Considering the visitation a punishment for the sins of his people, the sultan prohibited females from going outdoors and sought to make atonement by fresh exactions from Christians and Jews.

Exactions were not limited to non-Moslems. In the absence of a regulated system of taxation, the only way these sultans could raise enough money for their campaigns, extravagant courts and monumental buildings was by extortion from their subjects and from government officials who had enriched themselves at the expense of the public. Marauding Bedouins in the Delta and the desert to the east repeatedly fell on the settled *fallahin* of the narrow agricultural valley and ravaged the land. Locusts, like epidemics, made their periodic visitations. Famine became almost chronic and was intensified in the years of plague and drought caused by low water in the Nile. It is estimated that in the course of the Mamluk period the population of Syria and Egypt was reduced by two-thirds.

Toward the end of the period certain international factors began to contribute to the poverty and misery of the land. In 1497 to 1498 the Portuguese navigator Vasco da Gama found his way around the Cape of Good Hope. This was an event of vital importance in the history of the Syro-Egyptian kingdom. Not only did attacks from Portuguese and other European fleets become frequent on Moslem ships in the Red Sea and Indian waters but gradually most of the

247

traffic in spices and other tropical products of India and Arabia was diverted from Syrian and Egyptian ports and one of the main sources of national income forever destroyed.

An even greater barbarian than the Mamluks produced struck at Syria at the beginning of the fifteenth century. Timur Lang (name corrupted into Tamerlane) was born in 1336 in Transoxiana. One of his ancestors was vizir to Jenghiz's son, but the family claimed descent from Jenghiz himself. A satirical biographer, however, claims that Timur was the son of a shepherd and lived at first by brigandage and received the epithet Lang—"lame"—as a result of a wound inflicted on him while stealing sheep. In 1380 Timur at the head of his Tartar hordes initiated a long series of campaigns which gained for him Afghanistan, Persia, Faris and Kurdistan. In 1393 he captured Baghdad and in that and the following year overran Mesopotamia. In Takrit, the birthplace of Saladin, he erected a pyramid with the skulls of his victims. In 1395 he invaded the Volga River territory and occupied Moscow for over a year. Three years later he ravaged northern India and massacred 80,000 of the inhabitants of Delhi.

Like a cyclone Timur swept over northern Syria in 1401. For three days Aleppo was given over to plunder. The heads of over twenty thousand of its Moslem inhabitants were built into mounds ten cubits high by twenty in circumference, with all the faces on the outside. The city's priceless schools and mosques were destroyed,

never to be rebuilt. Hamah, Hims and Balabakk
fell in turn. The Egyptian army was routed
and Damascus captured. Its citadel held out for
a month. The city was sacked and committed to
the flames, and the invader—a nominal Moslem
with Shiite proclivities—extorted an opinion
from its religious leaders approving his conduct.
Of the Umayyad Mosque nothing was left but
the walls. From Damascus the wild conqueror
rushed back to Baghdad to avenge the deaths of
certain of his officers and dotted the city with a
hundred and twenty towers built of the heads
of the dead.

During the next two years Timur invaded
Asia Minor, crushed the Ottoman army at An-
kara on July 21, 1402, and took Sultan Bayazid
I prisoner. He even captured the capital, Brusa,
and Smyrna. Fortunately for the Mamluk kingdom, Timur died two years later while on the
march for a still more ambitious campaign
against China. His descendants exhausted themselves in internal struggles.

It was at the hands of the Ottomans, early in
the sixteenth century, that the Arab empire was
to receive its final blow. The Ottoman Turks
had originated in Mongolia, admixed with Iranian tribes in Central Asia and pressed into Asia
Minor, where they gradually displaced and
absorbed their Saljuq cousins and in the first
years of the fourteenth century established a
kingdom. The Ottoman problem began to con-
front the Egyptian sultans seriously in 1481.

Rivalry between the two powers found its
first expression in repeated conflicts among
their vassals on the borders of Asia Minor and
Syria. It developed slowly, and came to a head
in a battle between Mamluk and Turkish armies
near Aleppo on January 24, 1516. The Ottoman
victory was complete. The Turkish army was
better equipped with the new arms—artillery,
muskets and other long-range weapons—which
the Mamluk army, comprising Bedouin and
Syrian contingents, somewhat disdained to use.
The Turks had for some time been using pow-
der, but the Syro-Egyptians clung to the antiquated theory that personal valor is the decisive
factor in combat. Salim, the Ottoman sultan, entered Aleppo in triumph and was welcomed as a
deliverer from Mamluk excesses. Syria passed
into Ottoman hands, and from Syria the Ottoman conqueror swept south into Egypt. A year
later the Mamluk sultanate was forever crushed.
Cairo, the center of Eastern Islam since Saladin's
time, passed away as an imperial city and became
a provincial town. Mecca and Medina automati-
cally became a part of the Ottoman empire. The
Egyptian preachers who led the Friday public
services invoked Allah's blessing on Salim in the
following words:

"O Lord! uphold the sultan, son of the sultan,
ruler over both lands and the two seas, conqueror
of both hosts, monarch of the two Iraqs, minis-
ter of the two Holy Cities, the victorious king
Salim Shah. Grant him, O Lord, Thy precious
aid; enable him to win glorious victories, O

The Last Dynasty

Ruler of this world and the next, Lord of the universe."

Whether, as is alleged without sufficient warrant, the last puppet caliph made a transfer of his office to the Ottoman sultan or not, the fact remains that the Turkish ruler in Constantinople gradually absorbed the caliphal privileges and ultimately the title itself. Although some of Salim's successors styled themselves caliphs and were so addressed, their use of the title was only complimentary and unrecognized outside their own territories. The first known diplomatic document which applies the term caliph to the Ottoman sultan and recognizes his religious authority over Moslems outside of Turkey is the Russo-Turkish treaty of 1774.

The sultan-caliph of Constantinople became the most powerful potentate in Islam, an heir not only to the caliphs of Baghdad but also to the emperors of Byzantium. With the destruction of Mamluk power and the establishment of the Turks on the Bosphorus the focus of Islamic power shifted westward. The center of world civilization had moved to the West. The discovery of America and of the Cape of Good Hope had opened a new era. The history of the Arab caliphate and the Moslem dynasties that arose in medieval times on the ruins of the Arab empire came to an end. The Ottoman domination of the Arab world begins.

251

The Arab Lands in the Modern World

Medieval times, with their Dark Ages, held no blackout for the Arab lands; but modern times did. Throughout the four centuries of Ottoman domination, beginning in 1517, the whole Arab East was in a state of eclipse. Builders of one of the mightiest and most enduring of Moslem states, the Ottoman Turks conquered not only the Arab lands but the whole territory from the Caucasus to the gates of Vienna, dominated the Mediterranean area from their capital, Constantinople, and for centuries were a major factor in the calculations of Western European statesmen. In the meantime the once glamorous Medina, Damascus, Baghdad, Cairo, former capitals of mighty empires and brilliant seats of culture, receded into the background. They became residences for provincial governors and armed gar-

252

risons sent from Constantinople, the city before
whose walls had stood on four historic occasions
threatening Arab armies from Damascus and
Baghdad. The limelight now shone on the city
on the Bosphorus.

Besides Arabs the empire of the sultan-
caliphs embraced a heterogeneous mass of alien
nationalities, religious groupings and linguistic
units held together by the sword. The subjugated peoples shared in a common fate of excessive taxation and oppressive rule. No wonder if
under such conditions no creative work in art,
science or literature was produced by Arabic-
speaking peoples.

The Ottoman Empire, which reached its
height under Sulayman the Magnificent (1520-
1566), son of the conqueror of the Arab East,
started on its downward course immediately
after that. The course was long and tortuous.
After the unsuccessful attempt to capture
Vienna in 1683, the military role played by
Turkey was one of defense rather than offense.
The organization of the state for warfare rather
than peace, the vastness and unwieldiness of its
area, the heterogeneous character of its population, the persistence of the millet system where-
by religious communities enjoyed a large measure of home rule, the cleavage between Moslem
Turks and Moslem Arabs, the centralization of
the supreme authority in the hands of the sultan-
caliph and the ambiguity in the line of successorship—all these were serious inherent weaknesses
in the imperial setup. The internal forces of de-

cay and corruption were accelerated in the eighteenth century when neighboring and distant powers like Russia, Austria, France and England began to cast covetous eyes toward some possession of the "sick man" of Europe or pursue policies of special interest. The Arab world, once extending from Persia to Spain, inclusive, had by this time shrunk into its present dimensions. Persian nationality and language had reasserted themselves long before this. Spain was practically lost prior to the Turkish capture of Constantinople (1453). Northern Africa, Egypt, Arabia proper and the Arab Crescent—one contiguous region from the Atlantic to the Persian Gulf— retained their Arabic speech and Islamic character as they do at the present time. All these lands, with the exception of Morocco, formed until the early part of the nineteenth century part of the empire of the Turks. Lebanon was the only country to maintain through the ages a Christian majority.

First among the Arab lands to be detached from the empire was Algeria. It was occupied by the French in 1830 and later declared an integral part of France. Tunisia came next (1881) under French control. By 1912 France, Spain and Italy, the three Latin powers of Southern Europe, had established their ascendancy over the whole territory from Morocco to Libya. The fact that this whole North African block was the first to be detached from the Arab Moslem world and brought within the sphere of Western influence, together with the fact that its geographic position was peripheral to the lands of Islam and that its population had a large non-Arab element, served to denationalize its people and make them follow a course of their own. The heart and center of Arabism has always been in Western Asia and Egypt. Geographically a part of Africa, Egypt may be considered historically and culturally a part of Western Asia.

This block consisting of Western Asia and Egypt remained in name or reality in the embrace of the Ottoman Empire until the first World War. It was then that Egypt, which had been occupied by the British since 1882, cut the last tie with Constantinople. The Sharif Husayn of Mecca, a descendant of the Prophet, took advantage of the same opportunity to break with his Turkish suzerains. He moreover incited other Arabs to rise with him and meanwhile dreamed of a revived caliphate centering in Mecca with himself at its head. The "king of the Arabs" proclaimed himself in 1924, when Mustafa Kemal abolished the Ottoman caliphate, "caliph of the Moslems." This was the second essay at a modern Arab empire at the expense of Turkey, the first having been made in the thirties of the preceding century by Muhammad Ali, Egyptian viceroy and founder of the royal family which survived for almost a century and a half. Both essays were equally premature. They as yet had no solid foundation in the political consciousness of the people. Besides, they ran counter to British and other European interests in the Near East. Eventually Husayn lost even his hereditary domain, from which he was ousted by ibn-Saud, the shrewd and energetic head of the ultraconservative and puritanical Wahhabis of Najd. Between 1900 and 1925 this prince of the desert carved for himself a kingdom extending from the Persian Gulf to the Red Sea, the largest in the peninsula since the days of the Prophet. Saudi Arabia was so proclaimed in 1932. Its neighbor to the south, Yaman, was liberated from the Turkish yoke in the course of the first World War by its theocratic ruler the Imam Yahya, who was killed by a palace clique in 1948. Saudi Arabia and Yaman were the only fully independent states in the peninsula until 1961, when Kuwayt achieved its independence from Britain. Since then other states in eastern and southern Arabia have also freed themselves. Yaman and to a less extent Saudi Arabia have remained isolated and insulated against Western ideas. The tidal wave of modernization, global in dimensions, has somehow managed to by-pass their shores. The discovery and exploitation, in the last quarter of a century, of unequaled reservoirs of oil in the soil of Saudi Arabia, Kuwayt and Bahrayn enhanced the strategic importance of the area and fabulously enriched its rulers.

Subsequent to the first World War, a French mandate was inaugurated over Syria and Lebanon which was not shaken off until the end of the second World War. Palestine was mandated to Great Britain until 1948, when Israel was created against the will of the native inhabitants and despite the feeble resistance of all neighboring Arab states. Jordan, which began its political career as a part of the British mandate, was proclaimed a kingdom in 1946 under Abdullah, son of the Sharif Husayn of Hijaz and elder brother of Faysal. After a brief occupancy of the improvised throne of Syria, Faysal was overthrown by the French only to be installed (1921) by the British on the newly created throne of Iraq. Of the mandated territories Lebanon was the first to declare itself a republic; Iraq, though culturally behind Syria, was the first to free itself completely from the mandatory power and to achieve full independence. Iraq's declaration of independence was made in 1930. The bloody military coup of 1958, which substituted a republic for the monarchy, was the first of a series of leftist coups.

Of these lands Egypt was the first to feel the stirrings of a new life. The impulse came from the West; the occasion was the Napoleonic invasion of 1798. The French conqueror brought along with his other equipment an Arabic press which he had plundered from the Vatican and inaugurated with the aid of his savants a sort of *académie littéraire*. The first of its kind in the valley of the Nile, the press was succeeded by the famous Bulaq printing establishment, still a going concern.

Napoleon was followed by Muhammad Ali, father of modern Egypt, who, recognizing the possibilities of this abrupt contact between East and West, planned a followup He sent student

257

missions to Europe and invited European—
mainly French—missions to train officers and
scholars in Egypt.

When in 1831 this Egyptian viceroy, in pursuit
of his dream of an empire in Arab lands,
launched his campaign for the acquisition of
Syria, he opened the entire eastern border of the
Mediterranean to West European cultural influences. It was then that Protestant missionary enterprise—mainly American—established a firm
lodging there. The American Press at Beirut,
today capital of Lebanon, was founded in 1834.
It was the first adequately equipped press in
Syria. Three years later the native Protestant
church was organized. It was at that time that
the representatives of the Jesuit order returned
to Lebanon after a period of suspension. Their
Imprimerie Catholique was founded in Beirut in
1853. Both presses are still in operation and excel
in equipment. Two translations of the Bible into
modern Arabic were issued by them. English
and French works became numerous and popular in their Arabic editions. The American missionary activity culminated in the Syrian Protestant College (1866), now the American University of Beirut. Eight years later the Université
St. Joseph was installed on the other side of the
town. Until the present day these two institutions have maintained their position of educational leadership. Meantime numberless native
schools, printing presses, newspapers, magazines
and literary and scientific societies were instituted, especially in Lebanon.

This mountainous region bordering the sea had been oriented Westward as early as Phoenician, Roman and Byzantine days. Under two of its native princes, Fakhr-al-Din al-Ma'ni (1590-1635) and Bashir al-Shihabi (1786-1840), it achieved quasi-independence from Ottoman rule and meanwhile established vital cultural contacts with Italian, French and British institutions. Long before Muhammad Ali, the Lebanese Fakhr-al-Din had encouraged European traders, particularly French and Florentines, to found posts in Lebanon and invited agricultural missions from Tuscany. Both he and Bashir were exiled by the Porte from their native land and died in Constantinople, Fakhr-al-Din by violence.

After the civil war between Druzes and Maronites fomented by the Porte and culminating in the massacre of 1860, Lebanon enjoyed an autonomous regime—under a Christian governor —guaranteed by the great European powers. This measure of self-government safeguarded the continued flow of ideas and the application of stimuli from Western Europe. Since the population of the mountain was largely Christian, it was more predisposed for the reception of such concepts and more responsive to their stimuli. Many of its sons began to migrate after the mid-nineteenth century, as their early ancestors had done into all parts of the civilized world. Especially attractive to them was America, whence Lebanese and Syrian immigrants have forged a new channel for the conduct of modern liberal

259

The Arabs

ideas to the old homeland. Soon Lebanon out-
stripped all its neighbors in the race for modernization and secularization.

This impact of the West upon the East beginning with the early nineteenth century is the
most pregnant fact in its modern history. The
concomitant conflicts on the social, economic,
religious and intellectual levels are part of a fast
evolution from old societies to new ones. The
many serious and complicated problems of adjustment to the new life are far from being
solved.

Of the numberless ideas imported from the
West, the most dynamic were nationalism and
political democracy. The espousal of nationalism
led to the struggle for independence and constituted a definite break with the past.

Starting as a purely intellectual movement, the
Arab national awakening had for pioneers mostly
Syrian intellectuals, more specifically Christian
Lebanese, educated at the American University
of Beirut and operating in Egypt. The early
manifestations of the movement were revived
interest in classical Arabic, study of Arabic literature and research in Islamic history. Soon a consciousness of the past glory of the Arab empire
and of the cultural achievements and contributions of its citizens began to dawn upon the
literate body. The backward look suggested a
forward look. Political awakening followed intellectual awakening and the urge for a resusci-
tated, reunited Arab society began for the first

260

time to be strongly and widely felt. Political passivity gave way in favor of political activity.

The base from which this Arab nationalism started was a wide one. Its thesis was that all Arabic-speaking peoples—regardless of religion—were one people united through language and general culture. The attempt was one at Pan-Arabism rather than Pan-Islam. As it proceeded, however, the movement encountered serious local problems which served to divert its main course. In Egypt the first hurdle in the way was the British occupation of 1882. Opposition to the British rule began to absorb Egyptian interest and energy. Then and there Egyptian nationalism parted company with Pan-Arabism; it developed provincial, local aspects. For the first time in modern times the Egyptian came to realize that he was an Egyptian. "Egypt for the Egyptians" became the battle cry.

With the further fragmentation of the Arab East, consequent upon the first World War, Arab nationalism suffered further fragmentation. In Syria it concentrated its force against the policy of Turkification and, after the imposition of the mandate, against French imperialism. Similarly in Palestine hostility to the British mandate and its adjunct Zionism resulted in a local type of national feeling. Lebanon, which was first favorably disposed toward the mandate, ended by renouncing it vehemently and achieving full nationhood. The last mandatory vestiges were obliterated in Lebanon and Syria in 1943 to

1945. In the eastern horn of the Arab Crescent an Iraqi nationhood developed in the 1920's largely as a reaction against British imperialism. Tiny Transjordan, never an independent entity before, was amputated by the British in 1921 from South Syria and created a new state under the amir Abdullah.

Thus did these Arab component parts of the Ottoman Empire fall apart between the two world wars and develop into nations or quasi-nations. But the second World War and the threat of Zionism, which was viewed by Arabs everywhere as an intrusive movement, served to bring those parts once more closer together. The urge of common interest and the rising feeling of solidarity culminated in the Arab League, whose pact was signed in Cairo, March 1945. Original members included Egypt, Iraq, Saudi Arabia, Yaman, Lebanon, Syria and Jordan. Libya, Tunisia, Morocco, Sudan, Algeria and Kuwayt joined later. Jordan, Libya and Morocco are constitutional monarchies; Lebanon, Syria and Iraq are republics. All these states are now members of the United Nations and the majority have diplomatic representatives in Washington, London, Paris and other capitals of the world.

Originators of the third monotheistic religion, beneficiaries religiously and culturally of the other two, co-sharers with the West of the Greco-Roman tradition, holders aloft of the torch of enlightenment throughout medieval times, generous contributors to European renaissance, the Arabic-speaking peoples have thus taken their place among the forward-marching democratic nations of the world and promise to make further contributions to the progress of mankind. The achievement of the past is the promise of the present for the future.

Index

NAMES AND PLACES

265

Index

Euphrates, 4, 7, 107, 135, 136, 146, 163, 243

Fakhr-al-Din al-Ma'ni, 259
Far East, 114
Faraj ben-Salim, 143
Faris, 248
Fatimah, 39, 62, 77
Fatimid, 77, 195, 213, 214, 215, 219, 242, 243
Faysal, 257
Fazari, al-, 116, 117
Ferdinand of Aragon, 199, 200
Fertile Crescent, 7, 12, 20, 60, 71, 72, 117
France, 89, 90, 133, 166, 170, 177, 179, 220, 221, 254
Franks, 26, 91, 95, 164, 167, 220, 224 ff., 233 ff., 243
Frederick II, 208 ff.
Fustat, al-, 69

Gabriel, 32, 42, 49
Galen, 116, 119, 120, 141
Galicia, 85
Galicians, 167
Geber, 147, 148
Generalife, 171
Genoa, 220, 236
Georgia, 66
Gerard of Cremona, 143, 185
Germans, 166
Germany, 114, 166, 169, 191, 192, 209
Ghafiqi, al-, Abd-al Rah-man, 90 ff.
Ghalib, al-, Muhammad, 197
Gibraltar, 82, 92
Gindibu, 21
Gobi Desert, 10
Godfrey, 222

Golden Horde, 242
Good Hope, Cape of, 23, 247, 251
Gorze, 192
Gospels, 44, 243
Goths, 87 ff., 166, 202
Granada, 84, 176, 178 ff., 185, 197, 198, 200, 201, 204
Granada, University of, 178
Great Britain, 255, 256, 257
Great Khan, 218
Greece, 4, 7, 117, 141, 179, 204, 206, 262
Greeks, 8, 26, 72, 116, 117, 129

Hadramawt, v, 38
Hakam, al-, 172 ff.
Hamah, 218, 249
Hamites, 57, 81, 82, 194
Hammurabi, 20
Harun al-Rashid, 20, 109 ff., 120, 129, 130, 132, 137, 142, 152, 158, 159, 230, 242
Hasan, al-, 77, 78, 79
Hayyan, ibn-, Jabir, *see* Geber
Hazm, ibn-, 175
Hebrews, 7, 23-24, 74
Hellespont, 79
Heraclius, 65
Hijaz, 25, 28, 53, 64, 68, 87, 226, 243, 257
Hims, 95, 96, 249
Hippocrates, 119
Hirah, 118
Hittin, 225
Hittite-Hurrians, 7
Holy Grail, 233
Holy Land, 224
Holy Sepulchre, Church of the, 104, 110, 219, 220

Index

Hospitallers, 226
Hulagu, 217 ff., 239
Hunayn, ibn-Ishaq, 118 ff.
Husayn, King, 255 ff.

Ibrahim II, 204
Idrisi, al-, 208, 209
India, 7, 23, 63, 81, 114, 116, 136, 138, 139, 171, 235, 246, 248
Indonesia, 5, 54
Indus, 1, 80, 92, 106
Iran, 194
Iraq, v, 2, 7, 8, 9, 46, 53, 57, 65, 66, 67, 77, 80, 96, 116, 121, 128, 133, 135, 173, 185, 239, 257, 262
Isabella of Castille, 199
Isabelle of Brienne, 209
Isbahani, al-, 173
Islam, vi, 2, 5, 6, 13, 17 ff., 25 ff., 34 ff., 42-66, 96 ff., 108, 109, 115 ff., 132, 140, 156, 166, 174 ff., *et passim*
Ismailites, 195
Italy 7, 133, 166, 179, 204 ff., 210, 221, 254
Israel, 256

Jacobite, 157
Jaen, 170, 171
Jaffa, 231
Jahiliyah, 25, 26
Jahshiyari, al-, 152
James of Aragon, 242
Jassas, ibn-al-, 132
Jehovah, *see* Yahweh
Jenghiz Khan, 216, 217, 248
Jeremiah, 25
Jerusalem, 24, 33, 34, 36, 72, 86, 104, 155, 166, 222, 225, 226, 228, 230
Jesus, 44

Jews, 6, 31, 33, 34, 36, 37, 49, 52, 59, 72, 88, 89, 97, 118, 131, 137, 138, 190, 191, 225, 243, 247
Joannitius, *see* Hunayn ibn-Ishaq
Job, 44
John VIII, Pope, 205
Jordan, 2, 9, 257, 262
Judaism, vi, 5, 36, 41, 61
Judea, 116
Julius Caesar, 68, 70

Kaaba, 13, 30, 33, 36, 37, 50, 148
Karak, 226, 231
Kedar, 24
Khadijah, 31, 39
Khaldun, ibn-, 180, 181
Khalid ibn-al-Walid, 36, 57, 64, 65, 68
Kharijites, 55, 96
Khatib, ibn-al-, 180, 184
Khattab, ibn-al-, 20, 33, 34, 60, 64, 69, 70, 74
Khawlani, al-, al Samh, 90
Khayyam, al-, Umar, 145
Khurasan, 160
Khwarizmi, al-, 117, 146, 147, 149
Kindi, al-, 145
Koran, 13, 27, 30, 31, 32, 42-55, 59, 92, 100, 101, 130, 137, 138, 139, 150, 151, 152, 155, 157, 158, 178, 186, 192
Kufah, 133, 147
Kurdistan, 248
Kuwayt, v, 256, 262

La Fontaine, 175
League of Arab States, 4, 262
Lebanon, v, 2, 8, 9, 106, 124, 236, 254, 257 ff., 261, 262

Index

273

Index

1997 april

p. 51 supererogation

Edward ⊗ Said
Orientalism